READING AMERICAN HORIZONS

READING AMERICAN HORIZONS

PRIMARY SOURCES FOR U.S. HISTORY IN A GLOBAL CONTEXT
VOLUME II: SINCE 1865

FOURTH EDITION

Michael Schaller
UNIVERSITY OF ARIZONA

Janette Thomas Greenwood
CLARK UNIVERSITY

Andrew Kirk
UNIVERSITY OF NEVADA, LAS VEGAS

Sarah J. Purcell
GRINNELL COLLEGE

Aaron Sheehan-Dean
LOUISIANA STATE UNIVERSITY

Christina Snyder
PENNSYLVANIA STATE UNIVERSITY

NEW YORK   OXFORD
OXFORD UNIVERSITY PRESS

Oxford University Press is a department of the University of Oxford.
It furthers the University's objective of excellence in research, scholarship,
and education by publishing worldwide. Oxford is a registered trade mark of
Oxford University Press in the UK and certain other countries.

Published in the United States of America by Oxford University Press
198 Madison Avenue, New York, NY 10016, United States of America.

For titles covered by Section 112 of the US Higher Education
Opportunity Act, please visit www.oup.com/us/he for the latest
information about pricing and alternate formats.

Library of Congress Cataloging-in-Publication Data

Names: Schaller, Michael, 1947- author.
Title: Reading American horizons : primary sources for U.S. history in a
    global context / Michael Schaller, University of Arizona [and five
    others].
Other titles: Primary sources for U.S. history in a global context
Description: Fourth edition. | New York : Oxford University Press, [2021] |
    Includes bibliographical references. | Contents: Volume I. To 1877—
    Volume II. Since 1865. | Summary: "A higher education primary source
    book to accompany American Horizons: U.S. History in a Global Context,
    fourth edition."—Provided by publisher.
Identifiers: LCCN 2020008898 (print) | LCCN 2020008899 (ebook) | ISBN
    9780197531266 (v. 1 ; paperback) | ISBN 9780197530894 (v. 2 ; paperback)
    | ISBN 9780197530900 (v. 2 ; epub) | ISBN 9780197531259 (v. 1 ; epub)
Subjects: LCSH: United States—History—Sources.
Classification: LCC E178 .A5527 2021 (print) | LCC E178 (ebook) | DDC
    973—dc23
LC record available at https://lccn.loc.gov/2020008898
LC ebook record available at https://lccn.loc.gov/2020008899

Printing number: 9 8 7 6 5 4 3 2
Paperback printed by Marquis, Canada

CONTENTS

HOW TO READ A PRIMARY SOURCE

This sourcebook is composed of eighty-two primary sources. A primary source is any text, image, or other source of information that gives us a firsthand account of the past by someone who witnessed or participated in the historical events in question. While such sources can provide significant and fascinating insight into the past, they must also be read carefully to limit modern assumptions about historical modes of thought. Here are a few elements to keep in mind when approaching a primary source.

AUTHORSHIP

Who produced this source of information? A member of the elite or of the lower class? An outsider looking in at an event or an insider looking out? What's the author's gender? What's the author's cultural background? What profession or lifestyle does the author pursue, which might influence how he or she is recording the information?

GENRE

What type of source are you examining? Different genres—categories of material—have different goals and stylistic elements. For example, on the one hand, a personal letter meant exclusively for the eyes of a distant cousin might include unveiled opinions and relatively trivial pieces of information, like the writer's vacation plans. On the other hand, a political speech intended to convince a nation of a leader's point of view might subdue personal opinions beneath artful rhetoric and focus on large issues like national welfare or war. Identifying genre can be useful for deducing how the source may have been received by an audience.

AUDIENCE

Who is reading, listening to, or observing the source? Is it a public or private audience? National or international? Religious or nonreligious? The source may be geared toward the expectations of a particular group; it may be recorded in a language that is specific to a particular group. Identifying audience can help us understand why the author chose a certain tone or why he or she included certain types of information.

HISTORICAL CONTEXT

When and why was this source produced? On what date? For what purposes? What historical moment does the source address? It is paramount that we approach primary sources in context to avoid anachronism (attributing an idea or habit to a past era where it does not belong) and faulty judgment. For example, when considering a medieval history, we must take account of the fact that in the Middle Ages, the widespread understanding was that God created the world and could still interfere in the activity of mankind—such as sending a terrible storm when a community had sinned. Knowing the context (Christian, medieval, views of the world) helps us to avoid importing modern assumptions—like the fact that storms are caused by atmospheric pressure—into historical texts. In this way we can read the source more faithfully, carefully, and generously.

BIAS AND FRAMING

Is there an overt argument being made by the source? Did the author have a particular agenda? Did any political or social motives underlie the reasons for writing the document? Does the document exhibit any qualities that offer clues about the author's intentions?

STYLISTIC ELEMENTS

Stylistic features such as tone, vocabulary, word choice, and the manner in which the material is organized and presented should also be considered when examining a source. They can provide insight into the writer's perspective and offer additional context for considering a source in its entirety.

PREFACE

Reading American Horizons is a primary sources reader for the survey course in American history, designed to accompany the textbook *American Horizons*.

For more than four hundred years, North America has been part of a global network centered on the exchange of peoples, goods, and ideas. Human migrations—sometimes freely, sometimes forced—have continued over the centuries, along with the evolution of commerce in commodities as varied as tobacco, sugar, and computer chips. Europeans and Africans came or were brought to the continent, where they met, traded with, fought among, and intermarried with native peoples. Some of these migrants stayed, while others returned to their home countries. Still others came and went periodically. This initial circulation of people across the oceans foreshadowed the continuous movement of people, goods, and ideas that forged the United States. These forces shaped American history, both dividing and unifying the nation. American "horizons" truly stretch beyond our nation's borders, embracing the trading networks established during and after the colonial era to the digital social networks connecting people globally in the early twenty-first century.

Reading American Horizons uses primary source materials to help tell the story of the United States, by exploring this exchange on a global scale and placing it at the center of that story. By doing so, we provide a different perspective on the history of the United States, one that we hope broadens the horizons of those who read our work and is ever mindful of the global forces that increasingly and profoundly shape our lives. At the same time, *Reading American Horizons* considers those ways in which U.S. influence reshaped the lives and experiences of people of other nations.

Understanding documents and visual artifacts from the past is vital to the study of history. *Reading American Horizons* presents a selection of these materials, all carefully chosen to complement the narrative and themes presented in the accompanying *American Horizons*. It is our intention that students more deeply understand the historical narrative in the textbook by examining the original sources in this reader and that the contextual introductions and review questions enrich the interpretations we offer in the textbook.

What qualities make North America unique? What experiences did Americans share with other people around the globe? What accounts for the diversity of dialect and lifestyle across this country? How did the United States become a major player on the world stage of nations? History includes many storylines that contribute to this narrative. *Reading American Horizons* provides insight into the story of where this nation came from and how it has been shaped by its own set of shared values as well as its interaction with the rest of the world. *Reading American Horizons* depicts the intersection of storylines from many nations that influenced, and were influenced by, the United States of America.

As readers engage these materials, we encourage them to think explicitly about what makes history. What matters? What forces or events shaped how people lived their lives? What types of sources do historians rely on to explain the past? With all the sources in this book, readers should consider both what the creators hoped to accomplish and how people at the time might have read or viewed them. We encourage you to become your own historian, to read, analyze, and imagine the connections among the different voices that helped make the United States.

THE DEVELOPMENT STORY

The six coeditors of this book specialize in a variety of periods and methodologies. Based on our research and teaching, we all share the idea that the nation's history can best be understood by examining how, from the colonial era forward, the American experience reflected the interaction of many nations, peoples, and events. We present this idea in a format that integrates traditional narrative history with the enhanced perspective of five centuries of global interaction.

CHANGES TO THIS EDITION

Twenty-four new primary sources have been added the fourth edition, including fourteen new visual sources. These new sources provide a fuller picture of the global influences impacted by and on America:

CHAPTER 15:

- Visual Document: *And Not This Man?*
- Mississippi Black Codes (1865)
- Testimony of Elias Hill, Ku Klux Klan Hearings (1871)

CHAPTER 16:

- Visual Document: Reading the Images of Chinese Labor

CHAPTER 17:

- Visual Documents: The Pullman Strike: Two Political Cartoons (1894)

READING AMERICAN HORIZONS

RECONSTRUCTING AMERICA, 1865 TO 1877

15.1. JOURDON ANDERSON, LETTER TO P. H. ANDERSON (AUGUST 7, 1865)

Jourdon Anderson was one of the many ex-slaves who made their way north out of Tennessee and Kentucky into southern Ohio after the Civil War. The confused state of the labor market in the South led some masters to try to recruit former slaves back to their property to work as paid laborers.

Dayton, Ohio, August 7, 1865

To My Old Master, Colonel P. H. Anderson, Big Spring, Tennessee

Sir: I got your letter and was glad to find you had not forgotten Jourdon, and that you wanted me to come back and live with you again, promising to do better for me than anybody else can. I have often felt uneasy about you. I thought the Yankees would have hung you long before this for harboring Rebs they found at your house. I suppose they never heard about your going to Col. Martin's to kill the Union soldier that was left by his company in their stable. Although you shot at me twice before I left you, I did not want to hear of your being hurt, and am glad you are still living. It would do me good to go back to the dear old home again and see Miss Mary and Miss Martha and Allen, Esther, Green, and Lee. Give my love to them all, and tell them I hope we will meet in the better world, if not in this. I would have gone back to see you all when I was working in the Nashville Hospital, but one of the neighbors told me Henry intended to shoot me if he ever got a chance.

I want to know particularly what the good chance is you propose to give me. I am doing tolerably well here; I get $25 a month, with victuals and clothing; have a comfortable home for Mandy (the folks here call her Mrs. Anderson), and the children—Milly, Jane and Grundy—go to school and are learning well; the teacher says Grundy has a head for a preacher. They go to Sunday-School, and Mandy and me attend church regularly. We are kindly treated; sometimes we overhear others saying, "Them colored people were slaves"

Source: Lydia Maria Child, *The Freedmen's Book* (Boston: Ticknor and Fields, 1865), 265–67. Also see http://historymatters.gmu. edu/d/6369/.

down in Tennessee. The children feel hurt when they hear such remarks, but I tell them it was no disgrace in Tennessee to belong to Col. Anderson. Many darkies would have been proud, as I used to be, to call you master. Now, if you will write and say what wages you will give me, I will be better able to decide whether it would be to my advantage to move back again.

As to my freedom, which you say I can have, there is nothing to be gained on that score, as I got my free papers in 1864 from the Provost-Marshal-General of the Department of Nashville. Mandy says she would be afraid to go back without some proof that you are sincerely disposed to treat us justly and kindly; and we have concluded to test your sincerity by asking you to send us our wages for the time we served you. This will make us forget and forgive old scores, and rely on your justice and friendship in the future. I served you faithfully for thirty-two years and Mandy twenty years. At twenty-five dollars a month for me, and two dollars a week for Mandy, our earnings would amount to eleven thousand six hundred and eighty dollars. Add to this the interest for the time our wages has been kept back and deduct what you paid for our clothing and three doctor's visits to me, and pulling a tooth for Mandy, and the balance will show what we are in justice entitled to. Please send the money by Adams Express, in care of V. Winters, Esq., Dayton, Ohio. If you fail to pay us for faithful labors in the past we can have little faith in your promises in the future. We trust the good Maker has opened your eyes to the wrongs which you and your fathers have done to me and my fathers, in making us toil for you for generations

without recompense. Here I draw my wages every Saturday night, but in Tennessee there was never any payday for the Negroes any more than for the horses and cows. Surely there will be a day of reckoning for those who defraud the laborer of his hire.

In answering this letter please state if there would be any safety for my Milly and Jane, who are now grown up and both good-looking girls. You know how it was with Matilda and Catherine. I would rather stay here and starve, and die if it comes to that, than have my girls brought to shame by the violence and wickedness of their young masters. You will also please state if there has been any schools opened for the colored children in your neighborhood, the great desire of my life now is to give my children an education, and have them form virtuous habits.

P.S.—Say howdy to George Carter, and thank him for taking the pistol from you when you were shooting at me.

From your old servant,
Jourdon Anderson

QUESTIONS

1. What do Anderson's comments reveal about the economic knowledge of former slaves?
2. What are the attributes of freedom that Anderson identifies as most important?
3. Explain the new power dynamic between Anderson and his former master. How would each of the participants have understood it?

15.2. VISUAL DOCUMENT: *AND NOT THIS MAN?*

In his last speech before being assassinated, Abraham Lincoln suggested that the time had come to consider enfranchising black men, at least "the very intelligent, and on those who serve our cause as soldiers." This was a position that few white Northerners occupied at the start of the war, but Lincoln followed the changes produced by the conflict. Thomas Nast, one of the nation's most prominent political cartoonists, followed in August 1865 with the image here, published in the widely read *Harper's Weekly.*

Source: Nast, Thomas, Artist. Pardon. Franchise Columbia. - - "Shall I trust these men, and not this man?" / / Th. Nast. Confederate States of America United States, 1865. [New York: Harper's Magazine Co., August 5] Photograph. https://www.loc.gov/item/2010644408/.

QUESTIONS

1. What is the argument that Nast is making with this drawing?

2. How does presenting a soldier with a missing limb make a strong argument for enfranchising black men?

3. How would white Northerners likely have reacted to this message?

15.3. MISSISSIPPI BLACK CODES (1865)

In 1865, Southern states began rewriting their laws to account for emancipation. White Southerners made the barest minimum of concessions. They guaranteed that black people could marry, own property, and participate in legal proceedings (as witnesses and as defendants or plaintiffs). At the same time, most states also imposed new restrictions intended to curtail the freedom of black people. The "Black Codes" of Mississippi generated intense concern among Northerners.

Mississippi Apprenticeship Law:

... It shall be the duty of all sheriffs, justices of the peace, and other civil officers of the several counties in this State, to report to the probate courts of their respective counties semiannually, at the January and July terms of said courts, all freedmen, free negroes, and mulattoes, under the age of eighteen, in their respective counties, beats, or districts, who are orphans, or whose parent or parents have not the means or who refuse to provide for and support said minors; and thereupon it shall be the duty of said probate court to order the clerk of said court to apprentice said minors to some competent and suitable person on such terms as the court may direct, having a particular care to the interest of said minor: *Provided*, that the former owner of said minors shall have the preference when, in the opinion of the court, he or she shall be a suitable person for that purpose.

Mississippi Vagrancy Law:

... That all rogues and vagabonds, idle and dissipated persons, beggars, jugglers, or persons practicing unlawful games or plays, runaways, common drunkards, common night-walkers, pilferers, lewd, wanton, or lascivious persons, in speech or behavior, common railers and brawlers, persons who neglect their calling or employment, misspend what they earn, or do not provide for the support of themselves or their families, or dependents, and all other idle and disorderly persons, including all who neglect all lawful business, habitually misspend their time by frequenting houses of ill-fame, gaming-houses, or tippling shops, shall be deemed and considered vagrants, under the provisions of this act, and upon conviction thereof shall be fined not exceeding one hundred dollars . . . and be imprisoned, at the discretion of the court, not exceeding ten days.

QUESTIONS

1. Why would Northerners believe that the apprenticeship law was intended to reestablish slavery?
2. Why was the vagrancy law written so loosely? What would be the intent of arresting people who "neglect their calling" or "misspend what they earn?" Who decided when these conditions had been met?

Source: https://teachingamericanhistory.org/library/document/black-codes-of-mississippi/

15.4. GEORGES CLEMENCEAU, EXCERPT FROM AMERICAN RECONSTRUCTION, 1865–1870, AND THE IMPEACHMENT OF ANDREW JOHNSON (1867)

By late 1867, Andrew Johnson, a wartime Republican who ascended to the presidency after Lincoln's assassination, had alienated himself from congressional Republicans because of his conservative approach to Reconstruction. Johnson turned to Northern Democrats and Southerners (even though many remained disfranchised following the war) for support. Georges Clemenceau, a French physician and journalist, covered Washington politics for a French newspaper. He served as prime minister of France during the last year of World War I and helped draft the Treaty of Versailles.

September 10, 1867. The war between the President and Congress goes on, complicated from time to time by some unexpected turn. Contrary to all that has happened, is happening, and will happen in certain countries, the legislative power here has the upper hand. That is the peculiarity of the situation, or rather of this government. Congress may, when it pleases, take the President by the ear and lead him down from his high seat, and he can do nothing about it except to struggle and shout. But that is an extreme measure, and the radicals are limiting themselves, for the present, to binding Andrew Johnson firmly with good brand-new laws. At each session they add a shackle to his bonds, tighten the bit in a different place, file a claw or draw a tooth, and then when he is well bound up, fastened, and caught in an inextricable net of laws and decrees, more or less contradicting each other, they tie him to the stake of the Constitution and take a good look at him, feeling quite sure he cannot move this time.

But then Seward, the Dalila of the piece, rises up and shouts: "Johnson, here come the radicals with old Stevens at their head; they are proud of having subjected you and are coming to enjoy the sight of you in chains." And Samson summons all his strength, and bursts his cords and bonds with a mighty effort, and the Philistines (I mean the radicals) flee in disorder to the Capitol to set to work making new laws stronger than the old, which will break in their turn at the first test. This has been going on now for two years, and though in the course of things it is inevitable that Samson will be beaten, one must admit that he has put up a game fight. Even a sceptic, if this word has any meaning in America, would be interested in the struggle.

[. . .]

A new amnesty has been proclaimed for the former rebels in the South, and we shall soon see the struggle begin on a new point, that is, the interpretation to be given this proclamation of amnesty and the conclusions to be drawn from it. This is the second proclamation of amnesty which Mr. Johnson has issued. Though it still insists on the obligation to swear the oath of allegiance to the Constitution and the Union, it is infinitely more liberal in its terms than the first proclamation. Instead of the fourteen classes of exceptions defined in the proclamation of amnesty of May 29, 1865, the proclamation of September 8, 1867, defines only three. None are excluded from the benefits of amnesty except

Source: Georges Clemenceau, *American Reconstruction, 1865–1870, and the Impeachment of Andrew Johnson*, ed. Fernand Baldensperger (New York: Dial Press, 1928), 102–7.

the military and civil heads of the Confederate government, those who treated Federal prisoners contrary to the laws of warfare, and those who took part in the conspiracy which ended in the assassination of Lincoln. The *Tribune* estimated that the first proclamation left about one hundred thousand citizens out of the amnesty, and that this one leaves out one or two thousand. There is no harm done so far, but the question will be what are the exact rights conferred by the amnesty, in other words, whether the President has the power to reinstate the former rebels in their rights and to make voters of them. The President and the Democrats say *Yes*, Congress and the Republicans say *No*.

[. . .]

The Indians in the West have arrayed themselves against the whites, for the thousandth time. Massacres are being carried on by both sides, with brutal ferocity. The whites hunt down and drive the Indians as they formerly did the negroes in the South, and the Indians, in return, when they take prisoners, send them back to their relatives in pieces, without regard for age or sex. It is sad to be obliged to state that the first and real offenders are nearly always the white men.

QUESTIONS

1. How does Clemenceau characterize relations between the president and Congress?
2. How would Johnson's more liberal amnesty rules affect the landscape of postwar politics?
3. What connections were there between the Indian wars of the west and the Civil War?

15.5. TESTIMONY OF ELIAS HILL, KU KLUX KLAN HEARINGS (1871)

Embittered ex-Confederates organized the Ku Klux Klan in Tennessee in late 1865. Although the organization was mostly local, other white Southerners followed the same model. They used terrorism to suppress black political and social organization across the South. They targeted anyone associated with the Republican Party as well. In 1871, the federal government convened hearings to gather evidence about the atrocities committed in the region. A black man named Elias Hill gave the following testimony, which echoed that given by other witnesses. Hill suffered from rheumatism and had little use of his limbs, though he served as a Baptist preacher in his neighborhood in York County, South Carolina.

Supposed that it was them. They came in a very rapid manner and I could hardly tell whether it was the sound of horses or men. At last they came to my brother's door, which is in the same yard, and broke open the door and attacked his wife, and I heard her screaming and mourning. I could not understand what they said, for they were talking in an outlandish and unnatural tone, which I had heard they generally used at a negro's house. I heard them knocking around in her house. I was lying in my little cabin in the yard. At last I heard them have her in the yard. She was crying, and the Ku-Klux were whipping her to make her tell where I lived. I heard her say, "Yon is his house." She has told me since that they first asked who had taken

Source: Report of the Joint Select Committee to inquire into The Condition of Affairs in the Late Insurrectionary states (Washington, DC: Government Printing Office, 1872), 44-46. https://quod.lib.umich.edu/m/moa/ACA4911.0001.001.

me out of her house. They said, "Where's Elias?" She said, "He doesn't stay here; yon is his house." They were then in the yard, and I had heard them strike her five or six licks when I heard her say this. Some one then hit my door. It flew open. One ran in the house, and stopping about the middle of the house, which is a small cabin, he turned around, as it seemed to me as I lay there awake, and said, "Who's here?" Then I knew they would take me, and I answered, "I am here." He shouted for joy, as it seemed, "Here he is! Here he is! We have found him!" and he threw the bedclothes off of me and caught me by one arm, while another man took me by the other and they carried me into the yard between the houses, my brother's and mine, and put me on the ground beside a boy. The first thing they asked me was, "Who did that burning? Who burned our houses?"—gin-houses, dwelling-houses and such. Some had been burned in the neighborhood. I told them it was not me; I could not burn houses; it was unreasonable to ask me. Then they hit me with their fists, and said I did it, I ordered it. They went on asking me didn't I tell the black men to ravish all the white women. No, I answered them . . .

They caught me leg—you see what it is—and pulled me over the yard, and then left me there, knowing I could not walk nor crawl, and all six went into the house. I was chilled with the cold lying in the yard at that time of night, for it was near 1 o'clock, and they had talked and beat me and so on until half an hour had passed since they first approached. After they had staid in the house for a considerable time, they came back to where I lay and asked if I wasn't afraid at all. They pointed pistols at me, telling me they were going to kill me; wasn't I ready to die, and willing to die? Didn't I preach? That they came to kill me—all the time pointing pistols at me. This second time they came out of the house, after plundering the house, searching for letters, they came at me with these pistols, and asked if I was ready to die. I told them that I was not exactly ready; that I would rather live; that I hoped they would not kill me that time. They said they would; I had better prepare. One caught me by the leg and hurt me, for my leg for forty years has been drawn each year, more and more year by year, and I made moan when it hurt so. One said "G-d d—n it, hush!" He had a horsewhip, and he told me to pull up my

shirt, and he hit me. He told me at every lick, "Hold up your shirt." I made a moan every time he cut with the horsewhip. I reckon he struck me eight cuts right on the hip bone; it was almost the only place he could hit my body, my legs are so short—all my limbs drawn up and withered away with pain. I saw one of them standing over me motion to them to quit. They all had disguises on. I then thought they would not kill me. One of them took a strap, and buckled it around my neck and said, "Let's take him to the river and drown him." "What course is the river?" they asked me. I told them east. Then one of them went feeling about, as if he was looking for something, and said, "I don't see no east! Where is the d—d thing?" as if he did not understand what I meant. After pulling the strap around my neck, he took it off and gave me a lick on my hip where he had struck me with the horsewhip. One of them said, "Now, you see, I've burned up the d—d letter of Wallace's and all," and he brought out a little book and says, "What's this for?" I told him I did not know; to let me see with a light and I could read it. They brought a lamp and I read it. It was a book in which I had kept an account of the school. I had been licensed to keep a school. I read them some of the names. He said that would do, and asked if I had been paid for those scholars I had put down. I said no. He said I would now have to die. I was somewhat afraid, but one said not to kill me. They said "Look here! Will you put a card in the paper next week like June Moore and Sol Hill?" They had been prevailed on to put a card in the paper to renounce all republicanism and never vote. I said, "If I had the money to pay the expense, I could." They said I could borrow, and gave me another lick. They asked me, "Will you quit preaching?" I told them I did not know. I said that to save my life. They said I must stop that republican paper that was coming to Clay Hill. It has been only a few weeks since it stopped. The republican weekly paper was then coming to me from Charleston. It came to my name. They said I must stop it, quit preaching, and put a card in the newspaper renouncing republicanism, and they would not kill me; but if I did not they would come back next week and kill me. With that one of them went into the house where my brother and sister-in-law lived, and brought her to pick me up. As she stooped down to pick me up one of them struck her, and as she was carrying me into the house another struck her with a strap. She carried me into the house and laid me on the bed. Then they gathered around and told me to pray for them. I tried to pray. They said, "Don't you pray against Ku-Klux, but pray that God may forgive Ku-Klux. Don't pray against us. Pray that God may bless and save us." I was so chilled with cold lying out of doors so long and in such pain I could not speak to pray, but I tried to, and they said that would do very well, and all went out of the house except one. He handed me back a little book, that school-book, saying, "Here's that little book;" but it seemed that he forgot to speak in that outlandish tone, that they use to distinguish their voices. He spoke his common, plain voice, and then he went out.

QUESTION. Was that the end of it with you?

ANSWER. Yes, sir.

QUESTION. How many of these men were there?

ANSWER. Six.

QUESTION. How were they disguised?

ANSWER. With coverings over their faces. Some had a kind of check disguise on their heads. One had black oil-cloth over his head, and something like gloves covering his hands and wrists. When they brought the lamp to read that little book I could see his face all around his eyes, and he seemed a red-whiskered man.

QUESTION. Did you know any of them?

ANSWER. No, sir; I cannot say I know any one of them.

QUESTIONS

1. What is the purpose of the attack on Elias Hill?
2. Why would the Ku Klux Klan target a preacher?
3. What would the effect of this kind of attack be on Hill's community?

15.6. NORTH CAROLINA SHARECROPPING CONTRACT (JULY 21, 1882)

Beginning in 1865, freedpeople signed labor agreements with former plantation owners to share the growth and harvesting of cotton. Landholders granted access to the land and sharecroppers provided labor. Although sharecropping initially met the complementary needs of white and black Southerners in the first days of Reconstruction, the contracts exploited the landlessness of black Southerners and created a crisis of debt that trapped many farming families.

To every one applying to rent land upon shares, the following conditions must be read, and agreed to. To every 30 and 35 acres, I agree to furnish the team, plow, and farming implements, except cotton planters, and I do not agree to furnish a cart to every cropper. The croppers are to have half of the cotton, corn, and fodder (and peas and pumpkins and potatoes if any are planted) if the following conditions are complied with, but—if not—they are to have only two-fifths (2/5). Croppers are to have no part or interest in the cotton seed raised from the crop planted and worked by them. No vine crops of any description, that is, no watermelons, muskmelons, . . . squashes or anything of that kind, except peas and pumpkins, and potatoes,

Source: Grimes Family Papers (No. 3357), 1882, in the Southern Historical Collection, University of North Carolina at Chapel Hill. http://www.learnnc.org/lp/editions/nchist-newsouth/4765.

are to be planted in the cotton or corn. All must work under my direction. All plantation work to be done by the croppers. My part of the crop to be housed by them, and the fodder and oats to be hauled and put in the house. All the cotton must be topped about 1st August. If any cropper fails from any cause to save all the fodder from his crop, I am to have enough fodder to make it equal to one-half of the whole if the whole amount of fodder had been saved.

For every mule or horse furnished by me there must be 1000 good sized rails . . . hauled, and the fence repaired as far as they will go, the fence to be torn down and put up from the bottom if I so direct. All croppers to haul rails and work on fence whenever I may order. Rails to be split when I may say. Each cropper to clean out every ditch in his crop, and where a ditch runs between two croppers, the cleaning out of that ditch is to be divided equally between them. Every ditch bank in the crop must be shrubbed down and cleaned off before the crop is planted and must be cut down every time the land is worked with his hoe and when the crop is "laid by," the ditch banks must be left clean of bushes, weeds, and seeds. The cleaning out of all ditches must be done by the first of October. The rails must be split and the fence repaired before corn is planted.

[. . .]

All croppers must clean out stable and fill them with straw, and haul straw in front of stable whenever I direct. All the cotton must be manured, and enough fertilizer must be brought to manure each crop highly, the croppers to pay for one-half of all manure bought, the quantity to be purchased for each crop must be left to me.

No cropper is to work off the plantation when there is any work to be done on the land he has rented, or when his work is needed by me or other croppers. Trees to be cut down on Orchard, house field, & Evanson fences, leaving such as I may designate.

Road field is to be planted from the very edge of the ditch to the fence, and all the land to be planted close up to the ditches and fences. No stock of any kind belonging to croppers to run in the plantation after crops are gathered.

[. . .]

Every cropper must feed or have fed, the team he works, Saturday nights, Sundays, and every morning before going to work, beginning to feed his team (morning, noon, and night every day in the week) on the day he rents and feeding it to including the 31st day of December. If any cropper shall from any cause fail to repair his fence as far as 1000 rails will go, or shall fail to clean out any part of his ditches, or shall fail to leave his ditch banks, any part of them, well shrubbed and clean when his crop is laid by, or shall fail to clean out stables, fill them up and haul straw in front of them whenever he is told, he shall have only two-fifths (2/5) of the cotton, corn, fodder, peas, and pumpkins made on the land he cultivates.

[. . .]

Every cropper must be responsible for all gear and farming implements placed in his hands, and if not returned must be paid for unless it is worn out by use.

Croppers must sow & plow in oats and haul them to the crib, but must have no part of them. Nothing to be sold from their crops, nor fodder nor corn to be carried out of the fields until my rent is all paid, and all amounts they owe me and for which I am responsible are paid in full.

I am to gin & pack all the cotton and charge every cropper an eighteenth of his part, the cropper to furnish his part of the bagging, ties, & twine.

The sale of every cropper's part of the cotton to be made by me when and where I choose to sell, and after deducting all they owe me and all sums that I may be responsible for on their accounts, to pay them their half of the net proceeds. Work of every description, particularly the work on fences and ditches, to be done to my satisfaction, and must be done over until I am satisfied that it is done as it should be.

QUESTIONS

1. Why did the contract prohibit the growing of garden crops (watermelons, squash, etc.) on the land?
2. Why did the landholder claim the sole authority to sell whatever cotton was raised?
3. In what ways could sharecropping produce unexpected results for the sharecroppers?

CHAPTER 16

FORGING A TRANSCONTINENTAL NATION, 1877 TO 1900

16.1. FRANK H. MAYER WITH CHARLES B. ROTH, *THE BUFFALO HARVEST*

On the plains in the 1870s, cattle drives, ranching, overland migration, and depletion of resources contributed to the decline of the buffalo, but hunting and a short-lived but expansive world market for buffalo hides proved to be even more significant factors in the animal's near disappearance.

I found it out every day when I went out scouting for something to shoot. A couple of years before it was nothing to see[—]5,000, 10,000 buff[alo] in a day's ride. Now if I saw 50 I was lucky. Presently all I saw was rotting red carcasses or bleaching white bones. We had killed the golden goose.

During my runner's years I, quite naturally, wasn't interested in overall figures on total number killed, shipped, and so forth. I was a runner, not a statistician. But if I'd had sense enough in those days I could have realized in a few minutes' time that the game was on the way out. I couldn't have done anything about it, but I could have foreseen that my future was rather dim as a buffalo runner.

Completely accurate figures will likely never be compiled, but here are some authentic ones from the Southwest Historical Society which will show how thoroughly we killed the golden goose.

Dodge City, Kansas, was known as the buffalo city, and more hides were shipped from there than from anywhere else. The shipments started in earnest in 1871, but figures for that year are missing. During the winter of 1872–1873, one firm alone out of Dodge City shipped 200,000 hides. During the same year the same firm handled 1,617,000 pounds of buffalo meat, and $2,500,000 worth of buffalo bones. Now, that was big business in a small frontier town; and remember Dodge, although largest handler of buffalo hides and meat, was only one of a dozen cities that were on rails and shipping buffalo.

But notice how swiftly the traffic dropped. The buffalo years were only seven, 1871 to 1878. The last

Source: Frank H. Mayer with Charles B. Roth, *The Buffalo Harvest* (Chicago: Sage Press, 1958), 86–87.

big shipment was in 1878. It consisted of 40,000 hides, only a fifth of the number handled by the same firm from the same railhead seven years before. After that there weren't enough buffalo left to make handling profitable, so agents shut up their offices and got into some other racket, usually cattle, for fast on the heels of the buffalo came the cattle drives. Again Dodge assumed importance, took on a leading role.

Here are some other figures confirming the Dodge City figure I just cited.

In 1872, figures show that 1,491,489 buffalo were killed. In 1873, the high year, the figure given is 1,508,568. Now note this: in 1874, the total is only 158,583—the buffalo was decimated in just one year. Tragic picture, don't you think?

If you want to add the total killed during those three years you will see it comes to 3,158,730. But the Indian was getting his share, too, and Indian kills are set down by men who study records carefully enough to be listened to and believed, at 405,000 a year, or 1,215,000 in the three-year period.

Add the Indian crop to the white runners' crop and you will have a total kill for years 1872, 1873, and 1874 of 4,373,730 animals; in three years' time. No one can say how many were killed during the seven-year period the buffalo harvest lasted, but it must have been well over five million and might even have been close to six. Who knows?

I once, some years ago, sought a definite answer to that question by consulting railroads, because all the buffalo shipped from the ranges went by rail, and I figured if anyone would have the correct answer it would be the roads themselves. Everywhere I went I got the rather naive answer that the railroads couldn't answer my question, because they kept no records! Since when did railroads stop keeping records?

The Santa Fe got the lion's share of the business, and about a third of the hides went out over the Santa Fe. But the Santa Fe didn't keep records either, I was told!

What happens whenever the law of diminishing returns sets to work, increased efficiency, happened on the buffalo ranges. I know when I started in we were wasteful. We shot only cows. Their fur was softer; their skins were thinner; they were more in demand. If we killed a bull or two and we killed more than one or two just for the devil of it, we didn't bother to skin him; just left him lay for the wolves and coyotes to come along and do our job for us. Later on, we were glad to kill bulls, calves, anything.

We were wasteful of hides, too, and I have figures showing how we got over that and increased our efficiency in handling. In 1872, for instance, every hide that reached market represented three or four buffalo killed. The others were wasted by improper handling, rotting on the ground, and similar shiftlessnesses. The next year we began to tighten up a little: for every hide reaching railhead two buffalo gave their only lives. And in 1874, each hide represented the death of one and a-fourth buffalo. Yes, we became efficient, economical when we had nothing to be efficient or economical about. Our efficiency came too late. We learned our profession, but had no chance to practice it, which is always a tragedy.

One by one we runners put up our buffalo rifles, sold them, gave them away, or kept them for other hunting, and left the ranges. And there settled over them a vast quiet, punctuated at night by the snarls and howls of prairie wolves as they prowled through the carrion and found living very good. Not a living thing, aside from these wolves and coyotes stirred.

The buffalo was gone.

QUESTIONS

1. How does Mayer account for the wastefulness of the buffalo hunt?
2. According to Mayer, who or what was responsible for the destruction of the buffalo?
3. Why does he take the time to give such detailed figures?

16.2. JOHN WESLEY POWELL, EXCERPTS FROM *REPORT ON THE LANDS OF THE ARID REGION* (1879)

Starting in 1869, one-armed Civil War veteran John Wesley Powell led a series of important surveys of the Colorado River system. Setting out at Green River, Wyoming, in four boats, the Powell expedition followed the Colorado River through the Flaming Gorge, Desolation, Marble, and Grand Canyons, crossing the confluences of the Yampa, Green, and Little Colorado Rivers. In a second expedition in 1872, Powell explored the expansive Colorado Plateau. Powell was the first government scientist to understand the Colorado River's critical importance for the Southwest. His insightful 1879 *Report on the Lands of the Arid Region* recommended an alternative pattern of settlement based on his scientific findings about aridity. Powell warned that traditional settlement patterns and agricultural practices would fail in the arid West and counseled cautious settlement guided by hydrology and climate.

It was my intention to write a work on the Public Domain. The object of the volume was to give the extent and character of the lands yet belonging to the Government of the United States. Compared with the whole extent of these lands, but a very small fraction is immediately available for agriculture; in general, they require drainage or irrigation for their redemption.

It is true that in the Southern States there are some millions of acres, chiefly timber lands, which at no remote time will be occupied for agricultural purposes. Westward toward the Great Plains, the lands in what I have, in the body of this volume, termed the Humid Region have passed from the hands of the General Government. To this statement there are some small exceptions here and there—fractional tracts, which, for special reasons, have not been considered desirable by persons in search of lands for purposes of investment or occupation.

In the Sub-humid Region settlements are rapidly extending westward to the verge of the country where agriculture is possible without irrigation.

In the Humid Region of the Columbia the agricultural lands are largely covered by great forests, and for this reason settlements will progress slowly, as the lands must be cleared of their timber.

The redemption of the Arid Region involves engineering problems requiring for their solution the greatest skill. In the present volume only these lands are considered. Had I been able to execute the original plan to my satisfaction, I should have treated of the coast swamps of the South Atlantic and the Gulf slopes, the Everglade lands of the Floridian Peninsula, the flood plain lands of the great rivers of the south, which have heretofore been made available only to a limited extent by a system of levees, and the lake swamp lands found about the headwaters of the Mississippi and the region of the upper Great Lakes. All of these lands require either drainage or protection from overflow, and the engineering problems involved are of diverse nature. These lands are to be redeemed from excessive aridity. When the excessively humid lands are redeemed, their fertility is almost inexhaustible, and the agricultural capacity of the United States will eventually be largely increased by the rescue of these lands from their present valueless condition. In like

Source: John Wesley Powell, *Report on the Lands of the Arid Region of the United States* (Washington, DC: U.S. Government Printing Office, 1879).

manner, on the other hand, the arid lands, so far as they can be redeemed by irrigation, will perennially yield bountiful crops, as the means for their redemption involves their constant fertilization.

To a great extent, the redemption of all these lands will require extensive and comprehensive plans, for the execution of which aggregated capital or cooperative labor will be necessary. Here, individual farmers, being poor men, cannot undertake the task. For its accomplishment a wise prevision, embodied in carefully considered legislation, is necessary. It was my purpose not only to consider the character of the lands themselves, but also the engineering problems involved in their redemption, and further to make suggestions for the legislative action necessary to inaugurate the enterprises by which these lands may eventually be rescued from their present worthless state. When I addressed myself to the broader task as indicated above, I found that my facts in relation to some of the classes of lands mentioned, especially the coast swamps of the Gulf and some of the flood plain lands of the southern rivers, were too meager for anything more than general statements. There seemed to be no immediate necessity for the discussion of these subjects; but to the Arid Region of the west thousands of persons are annually repairing, and the questions relating to the utilization of these lands are of present importance. Under these considerations I have decided to publish that portion of the volume relating to the arid lands, and to postpone to some future time that part relating to the excessively humid lands. . . .

In the preparation of the contemplated volume I desired to give a historical sketch of the legislation relating to swamp lands and executive action thereunder; another chapter on bounty lands and land grants for agricultural schools, and still another on land grants in aid of internal improvements—chiefly railroads. The latter chapter has already been prepared by Mr. Willis Drummond, jr., and as the necessary

map is ready I have concluded to publish it now, more especially as the granted lands largely lie in the Arid Region. Mr. Drummond's chapter has been carefully prepared and finely written, and contains much valuable information.

To the late Prof. Joseph Henry, secretary of the Smithsonian Institution, I am greatly indebted for access to the records of the Institution relating to rainfall. Since beginning my explorations and surveys in the far west, I have received the counsel and assistance of the venerable professor on all important matters relating to my investigations; and whatever of value has been accomplished is due in no small part to his wisdom and advice. I cannot but express profound sorrow at the loss of a counselor so wise, so patient, and so courteous.

I am also indebted to Mr. Charles A. Schott, of the United States Coast Survey, to whom the discussion of the rain gauge records has been intrusted by the Smithsonian Institution, for furnishing to me the required data in advance of publication by himself. Unfortunately, the chapters written by Messrs. Gilbert, Dutton, Thompson, and Drummond have not been proof-read by themselves, by reason of their absence during the time when the volume was going through the press; but this is the less to be regretted from the fact that the whole volume has been proof-read by Mr. J. C. Pilling, whose critical skill is all that could be desired.

QUESTIONS

1. Why does Powell think that rainfall is an important consideration for the settlement of the West?
2. Who might be capable of achieving the "extensive and comprehensive plans" needed to make the arid West agriculturally productive and suitable for settlement?
3. Who does he indicate is not able to achieve these plans alone?

16.3. *SOUTHERN WORKMAN AND HAMPTON SCHOOL RECORD* AND EDNA DEAN PROCTOR, "COLUMBIA'S ROLL CALL" (JUNE 1892) AND "THE INDIANS' APPEAL" (JANUARY 1892)

The establishment of Indian boarding schools became an official U.S. policy with the passage of the Dawes Act on February 8, 1887. Indian education was a simple idea proposed by reformers who thought they were providing a humanitarian alternative to violence. Indian children were taken away from their "ignorant" parents and "backward" communities and trained to be Americans who cherished individualism and republicanism over tribal life. Indian boarding schools commemorated the passage of the Dawes Act with a special holiday and an elaborate pageant designed to reinforce the ideals of Indian assimilation. The Hampton School celebrated with a stage production, "Columbia's Roll Call."

COLUMBIA'S ROLL CALL

The platform was cleared for the scenic representation of "Columbia's Roll Call," a reproduction, with some abbreviation, of that given on Indian Citizenship day, of which our March number contained a full account. The characters were taken by the same students as then, so far as possible, and they entered into it with equal spirit. Juanita presided with queenly dignity as Columbia, "from her century terraced height;" the heroes who had made her great, summoned forth from the past by the Heralds of Fame and History, took their stand at her right hand—Columbus, Capt. John Smith; Miles Standish and the Puritan maiden; John Elliot, Apostle to the Indians, William Penn and a sister of peace, and the great Washington. Again the "Indian Petitioner" threw herself at the foot of the throne, beseeching a share for her people with Columbia's children, and, to justify her plea, Fame and History summoned those who could balance the roll of pale face heroes—the friend of Columbus from San Salvador; Pocahontas the savior of Capt. John Smith, Samoset, welcomer of the pilgrims; one of Eliot's Indian converts; Taminend, friend of William Penn, and the White Mingo, friend of Washington. The double line of heroes, in the varied beautiful costumes of the old world and the wilderness, made a brilliant setting for Columbia's throne, the keystone of the arch. Every word spoken by the characters was distinct and clear, and very sweetly the voices of the Pilgrims blended in Mrs. Heman's song of "The Breaking Waves Dashed High." But Columbia was not satisfied with past records. Had she not conferred her citizenship already on one other race? The Afro-American Student of Hampton stepped forward with the stars and stripes. What can the petitioner match with that? She is ready with "The Hampton Indian Student," who bearing the School's banner took stand opposite. "This is well for the present, what of the future?" "Who is ready to pledge our future?" "Speak for yourselves?" A rush from the ranks of the Indian school, and gathering under the Hampton flag they respond, in the song, "Spirit of Peace." "Brothers, we come at your altars to pray." "It is enough. Take my banner," says Columbia, "and your place as my citizens." "Speed our Republic,

Sources: "Columbia's Roll Call," *Southern Workman and Hampton School Record* 21, no. 6 (June 1892), 82; and Edna Dean Procter, "The Indians' Appeal," *Southern Workman and Hampton School Record* 21, no. 1 (January 1892), 11.

O Father on High!" What can close the scene but a general chorus of "My Country, 'tis of Thee." The Indian actors linger to listen to a representative of whom they may well be proud. A fitting close and beautiful addition to the tableau of Columbia's Roll Call was made, as before the half-circle of brilliantly costumed heroes of the past of two races, stepped the dignified, erect, high-souled woman, the representative and product of the best progress of one, the best philanthropy of the other—LaFlesche, the Arrow— Arrow of the Future from the bow of the Past strained by the cord of the Present.

THE INDIANS' APPEAL

You have taken our rivers and fountains And the
    plains where we loved to roam,—
Banish us not to the mountains
And the lonely wastes for home!
No! let us dwell among you;
Cheer us with hope again;
For the life of our fathers has vanished,
And we long by your side to be men.
Our clans that were strongest and bravest
Are broken and powerless through you;
Let us join the great tribe of the white men,
As brothers to dare and to do!
We will fight to the death in your armies;

As scouts we will distance the deer
Trust us, and witness how loyal
Are the ranks that are stranger to fear!
And the still ways of peace we would follow—
Sow the seed and the sheaves gather in,
Share your labor, your learning, your worship,
A life larger, better, to win.
Then, foeman no longer nor aliens,
But brothers indeed we will be,
And the sun find no citizens truer
As he rolls to the uttermost sea.
You have taken our rivers and fountains
And the plains where we loved to roam,—
Banish us not to the mountains
And the lonely wastes for home!
No! let us dwell among you;
Cheer us with hope again;
For the life of our fathers has vanished,
And we long by your side to be men.

QUESTIONS

1. What was the message of Indian Citizenship Day?
2. What does the first passage ask of the students who recited these words?
3. What do Anglo-American attempts to reform Native American peoples imply about the former's view of themselves?

16.4. VISUAL DOCUMENT: READING THE IMAGES OF CHINESE LABOR

Throughout the history of the transcontinental enterprise, Chinese immigrants were recognized only as "John Chinaman" or "Crocker's Chinese pets," remaining individually nameless despite numbering in the tens of thousands and often making up 90 percent of the workforce. Chinese immigrants also built cities and towns across the West, establishing some of the most lasting immigrant ethnic communities in the United States. Despite significant and lasting legacies, researching this important group can sometimes be difficult and require analysis of a range of sources, including photographs.

317. End of Track,

on Humboldt Plains.

QUESTIONS

1. Who are the people in this image? What else do you notice in the frame that is of interest to historians?

2. What can we learn by studying these people and their places in this photograph?

3. How can a photograph be used as historical evidence?

Source: End of Track, on Humboldt Plains (Stanford Special Collections. https://searchworks.stanford.edu/view/nc812bv0419)

CHAPTER 17

A NEW INDUSTRIAL AND LABOR ORDER, 1877 TO 1900

17.1. EMMA E. BROWN, EXCERPTS FROM "CHILDREN'S LABOR: A PROBLEM" (DECEMBER 1880)

One of the most industrialized states in the country, Massachusetts passed several child labor laws in the nineteenth century limiting the employment of children. The law made it illegal to employ children under the age of ten and established educational requirements, including mandatory certification from school committees, for employed children between the ages of ten and fourteen. In 1880, journalist Emma E. Brown reported on the effectiveness of the law in an article published in the *Atlantic Monthly*.

During the past year some hundred and sixty factories in the State that had been inspected give an average of only two percent where strict compliance was found. . . . In one factory the inspector was shown a file of certificates which gave the names of thirteen children employed in the mills, but no data on their ages. Singling out, at random, a bright little fellow busily at work as a "doffer," the inspector asked him his name and age. "John Donnelly, sir, and I'm goin' on twelve years," was the ready response.

"But how is this?" said the officer, running over the list of certificates he still held in his hand. "There's no such name here as 'John Donnelly' and—Well, who is that little girl tubing the machine by the window?"

"Oh, her's Maggie Sweeney," said the little doffer, thrusting a huge square of tobacco into his mouth and hurrying back to his work, as if to avoid further questioning.

No Maggie Sweeney, either, was to be found among the names on the certificates, and the officer's suspicions being now fully aroused, he questioned a number of little operatives, whereupon it appeared that *not one half* of the children employed in the factory were represented upon the certificates. Further investigation also proved that a large proportion of these children were under ten years of age. . . .

In another factory, where the certificates seemed to show a compliance with the laws, a fine, well-developed girl of fourteen was found who could

Source: Emma E. Brown, "Children's Labor: A Problem," *Atlantic Monthly*, December 1880, 787–92.

neither read nor write. "She had worked in the mills ever since she could remember,—had *never had no time* to go to school."

In still another factory, the very first child interviewed was under ten years of age. . . .

Systematic investigation has shown that of the 13,000 children employed in various factories throughout the State in 1878 only 4575 received the legal amount of schooling; and that among the 282,485 children in Massachusetts between the ages of five and fifteen there are no less than 25,000 children who never have been present in either our public or private schools.

An overseer in one of the print works in the State says: "There seems to be a growing disposition on the part of parents to put their children to work before they are of the legal age, and to avoid sending them to school the length of time required by law. Scarcely a day passes but mothers come to the mills and beg us to use our influence in procuring employment for their children."

"We endeavor to comply with the school law," said a prominent mill owner to one of the inspectors, "but find it extremely difficult, as parents again and again give false statements regarding their children's ages." . . .

"Please, sir, could Denise have a permit to stay in the mills a month longer? It's time she was in school, I know but the father is all drawn up with rheumatis', and they've took him to the 'ospital, and I don't know how ever in the world we're goin' to git along if Denise has to leave the mills!"

It was all said in one breath, and the superintendent of the schools, glancing up from his books, saw a woman of thirty-five or thereabouts, with a peculiar, dazed expression, and eyes as dull and faded as the old gray waterproof she was nervously twitching with one finger.

He answered, not unkindly, "We cannot give any such permit. Besides, you are liable to a fine of fifty dollars, if the child is kept out of school. How old did you say she was?"

"Eleven years, sir." . . .

"Has she ever been to school?"

"Oh, yes, sir. Tell the gentleman, Denise, what reader you were in last."

"'Twas the First Reader,—the primer, you know," whispered the little girl, hanging down her head.

"A child of eleven years ought to be farther advanced than that!" remarked the superintendent.

"I suppose so," acknowledged the mother, with a sigh; "but I couldn't spare her to go to school when she was a earnin' twenty cents a day."

"Has your husband been a drinking man?"

"Oh, no. Not but that he would take a glass, now and then, but it never got the better of him,—oh no! He's always been a good husband, and we got along nicely whilst he was well and a gittin' fair wages. Denise never worked a day in the mills, sir, till the rheumatis' took *him*. He was a shoemaker by trade, and I've been a takin' in sewing, off and on, as I could git it; but work is scarce now, sir, and they say at the 'ospital as how he may never be able to use his hands agin, sir, and it's more nor I know what ever's a goin' to become of us! . . ."

The superintendent shook his head. "I am really very sorry for you, madam, but according to the law your little girl must enter school to-morrow." . . .

My friend, who had happened in at the superintendent's office and heard the whole conversation, resolved to investigate the case. She found the woman's story true in every particular. . . .

My friend left the office in a brown study. "Can it be a normal state of things," she said to a certain political economist, "when children of eleven years are reckoned among the bread winners of a State?"

"Something must be wrong," he answered, "when an organic law of production is violated, as is the case in Massachusetts, where children between the ages of ten and fifteen constitute forty-four percent of the whole number of working people, and yet produce but twenty-four percent of the income!"

"But is it not possible for a strong, able-bodied man, if he is temperate and provident, to earn enough to support his family and keep his children in school till they are fifteen?"

"It certainly ought to be, but with the present relation of wages to cost of living in Massachusetts it seems that a laboring man with a family cannot keep out of debt with a yearly income of *less* than $600. Now, the fact is that the majority of workingmen earn less than $600 a year. I know of one Irish family where both the father and eldest son, a child of about twelve, work in the mills. Their combined earnings amount to $564.... The family numbers six, and one of the four children the parents have kept in school. They dress shabbily, occupy a tenement of four rooms in one of the most unhealthy localities in the city, and are in a wretched condition generally. Knowing that the family were constantly running in debt, I inquired into their items of expense, and found the yearly amount to be [$589]. . . . This total of $589 is a larger expenditure than is warranted by the income of $564. Subtract from this income the child's wages, which amount to $132, and you find the father's income to be only $432. What would be the financial condition of this family without the child's labor? I cannot tell how provident they are, but it is difficult to see where their expenses could be lessened." . . .

"It would seem, then, that without children's assistance, other things remaining equal, the majority of workingmen's families in Massachusetts would be in poverty or in debt?"

"That would seem, indeed, to be the true statement of the case."

In England, the over-working and under-schooling of minors is now a subject of heavy penalties; but past generations of factory children have already given rise to an almost distinct class of English working people,—pale, sallow, and stunted both in physical and mental growth.

How long will it be before a deteriorated race like the Stockinger, Leicester, and Manchester spinners springs up on our New England soil?

QUESTIONS

1. How would the author of this article answer her own question regarding child labor: "Who is to blame"?

2. According to the author, what are the short-term and long-term consequences of child labor?

3. How would an industrialist of this era have responded to this article?

17.2. ANDREW CARNEGIE, "GOSPEL OF WEALTH" (JUNE 1889)

Millionaire industrialist Andrew Carnegie published "Wealth" in 1889, and its arguments, justifying the benefits of capitalism and the responsibility of the wealthy to give away their fortunes before death, soon became known as "The Gospel of Wealth."

The problem of our age is the proper administration of wealth, that the ties of brotherhood may still bind together the rich and poor in harmonious relationship. The conditions of human life have not only been changed, but revolutionized, within the past few hundred years. In former days there was little difference between the dwelling, dress, food, and environment of the chief and those of his retainers. . . . The contrast between the palace of the millionaire and the cottage of the laborer with us to-day measures the change which has come with civilization. This change, however, is not to be deplored, but welcomed as highly beneficial. It is well, nay, essential, for the progress of the race that the houses of some should be homes for all that is highest and best in literature and the arts, and for all the refinements of civilization, rather than that none should be so. Much better this great irregularity than universal squalor. . . . The "good old times" were not good old times. Neither master nor servant was as well situated then as to-day. A relapse to old conditions would be disastrous to both—not the least so to him who serves—and would sweep away civilization with it. But whether the change

Source: Andrew Carnegie, "Wealth," *North American Review* (June 1889): 653–55.

be for good or ill, it is upon us, beyond our power to alter, and, therefore, to be accepted and made the best of. It is a waste of time to criticize the inevitable. . . .

We start, then, with a condition of affairs under which the best interests of the race are promoted, but which inevitably gives wealth to the few. . . . The question then arises . . . What is the proper mode of administering wealth after the laws upon which civilization is founded have thrown it into the hands of the few? And it is of this great question that I believe I offer the true solution. . . .

There are but three modes in which surplus wealth can be disposed of. It can be left to the families of the decedents; or it can be bequeathed for public purposes; or, finally, it can be administered by its possessors during their lives. Under the first and second modes most of the wealth of the world that has reached the few has hitherto been applied. Let us in turn consider each of these modes. The first is the most injudicious. . . . Why should men leave great fortunes to their children? If this is done from affection, is it not misguided affection? Observation teaches that, generally speaking, it is not well for the children that they should be so burdened. Neither is it well for the State. Beyond providing for the wife and daughters moderate sources of income, and very moderate allowances indeed, if any, for the sons, men may well hesitate; for it is no longer questionable that great sums bequeathed often work more for the injury than for the good of the recipients. Wise men will soon conclude that, for the best interests of the members of their families, and of the State, such bequests are an improper use of their means. . . .

As to the second mode, that of leaving wealth at death for public uses, it may be said that this is only a means for the disposal of wealth, provided a man is content to wait until he is dead before he becomes of much good in the world. Knowledge of the results of legacies bequeathed is not calculated to inspire the brightest hopes of much posthumous good being accomplished by them. . . . In many cases the bequests are so used as to become only monuments of his folly. It is well to remember that it requires the exercise of not less ability than that which acquires it, to use wealth so as to be really beneficial to the community. . . .

There remains, then, only one mode of using great fortunes; but in this we have the true antidote for the temporary unequal distribution of wealth, the reconciliation of the rich and the poor—a reign of harmony,

another ideal, differing, indeed, from that of the Communist in requiring only the further evolution of existing conditions, not the total overthrow of our civilization. It is founded upon the present most intense Individualism, and the race is prepared to put it in practice by degrees whenever it pleases. Under its sway we shall have an ideal State, in which the surplus wealth of the few will become, in the best sense, the property of the many, because administered for the common good; and this wealth, passing through the hands of the few, can be made a much more potent force for the elevation of our race than if distributed in small sums to the people themselves. Even the poorest can be made to see this, and to agree that great sums gathered by some of their fellow-citizens and spent for public purposes, from which the masses reap the principal benefit, are more valuable to them than if scattered among themselves in trifling amounts through the course of many years. . . .

This, then, is held to be the duty of the man of wealth: To set an example of modest, unostentatious living, shunning display or extravagance; to provide moderately for the legitimate wants of those dependent upon him; and, after doing so, to consider all surplus revenues which come to him simply as trust funds, which he is called upon to administer, and strictly bound as a matter of duty to administer in the manner which, in his judgment, is best calculated to produce the most beneficial results for the community—the man of wealth thus becoming the mere trustee and agent for his poorer brethren, bringing to their service his superior wisdom, experience, and ability to administer, doing for them better than they would or could do for themselves. . . .

The best uses to which surplus wealth can be put have already been indicated. Those who would administer wisely must, indeed, be wise; for one of the serious obstacles to the improvement of our race is indiscriminate charity. It were better for mankind that the millions of the rich were thrown into the sea than so spent as to encourage the slothful, the drunken, the unworthy. Of every thousand dollars spent in so-called charity to-day, it is probable that nine hundred and fifty dollars is unwisely spent—so spent, indeed, as to produce the very evils which it hopes to mitigate or cure. . . .

In bestowing charity, the main consideration should be to help those who will help themselves; to provide part of the means by which those who desire to improve may do so; to give those who desire to rise the aids by which they may rise; to assist, but rarely or never to do all. Neither the individual nor the race is improved by almsgiving. Those worthy of assistance, except in rare cases, seldom require assistance. The really valuable men of the race never do, except in case of accident or sudden change. . . .

The rich man is thus almost restricted to following the examples of Peter Cooper, Enoch Pratt of Baltimore, Mr. Pratt of Brooklyn, Senator Stanford, and others, who know that the best means of benefiting the community is to place within its reach the ladders upon which the aspiring can rise—free libraries, parks, and means of recreation, by which men are helped in body and mind; works of art, certain to give pleasure and improve the public taste; and public institutions of various kinds, which will improve the general condition of the people; in this manner returning their surplus wealth to the mass of their fellows in the forms best calculated to do them lasting good.

Thus is the problem of rich and poor to be solved. The laws of accumulation will be left free, the laws of distribution free. Individualism will continue, but the millionaire will be but a trustee for the poor, in-trusted for a season with a great part of the increased wealth of the community, but administering it for the community far better than it could or would have done for itself. The best minds will thus have reached a stage in the development of the race in which it is clearly seen that there is no mode of disposing of surplus wealth creditable to thoughtful and earnest men into whose hands it flows, save by using it year by year for the general good. This day already dawns. Men may die without incurring the pity of their fellows, still sharers in great business enterprises from which their capital cannot be or has not been withdrawn, and which is left chiefly at death for public uses; yet the day is not far distant when the man who dies leaving behind him millions of available wealth, which was free to him to administer during life, will pass away "unwept, unhonored, and unsung," no matter to what uses he leaves the dross which he cannot take with him. Of such as these the public verdict will then be: "The man who dies thus rich dies disgraced."

Such, in my opinion is the true gospel concerning wealth, obedience to which is destined some day to solve the problem of the rich and the poor, and to bring "Peace on earth, among men good will."

QUESTIONS

1. What are the three ways, according to Carnegie, that wealth can be distributed? Which is best in his opinion? Why?
2. What is "the duty" of the man of wealth?
3. What kinds of charities and support are best? Who should be the recipients of these charities?

17.3. VISUAL DOCUMENTS: THE PULLMAN STRIKE: TWO POLITICAL CARTOONS (1894)

These political cartoons—one from the *Harper's weekly* and the other from *Chicago Labor Newspaper*, both published in July 1894, reflect the deep division among Americans regarding the Pullman Strike as well as the use of strikes by labor unions.

THE VANGUARD OF ANARCHY.

THE CONDITION OF THE LABORING MAN AT PULLMAN. —

QUESTIONS

1. What is each cartoonist's point of view regarding the Pullman Strike?

2. What symbols does each cartoonist use to make his point?

3. How are working people depicted in each cartoon?

Source: Chicago Labor Newspaper, July 7, 1894./Wikipedia

17.4. TWO VIEWS OF THE HOMESTEAD LOCKOUT: EXCERPTS FROM *THE MANUFACTURER AND BUILDER* (AUGUST 1892) AND *NEW ENGLAND MAGAZINE* (SEPTEMBER 1892)

Americans drew different conclusions about the violent Homestead Lockout that occurred in 1892 and the subsequent victory of Carnegie Steel over its union workers. The following two editorials represent two opposing views. The first of these editorials was published in *The Manufacturer and Builder*, which, as its name suggests, was a trade journal for industrialists and other businessmen. The second editorial was published in *New England Magazine*, which was a general-interest illustrated monthly published in Boston.

THE HOMESTEAD AFFAIR

As indicated last month in our comments on the Homestead incident, the conflict is virtually ended, and the works are now being operated by non-union workmen. The disappointed and desperate leaders of the subdued rioters, it is true, continue to talk of the fight for the recognition of their union as still going on, but this silly opposition to the logic of facts deceives no one but the more ignorant and unthinking of the rank and file of their following. In fact, the fight was lost to the men from the moment when they placed themselves, at the outset, in the position of law-breakers, and gave the American people an object lesson in the practical application of the principles of trades unionism, which they are not likely soon to forget. On the whole, and barring the reckless sacrifice of human life involved in this episode, it may prove in the end to be a blessing, if it shall teach the greatly-needed lesson to the authorities everywhere throughout the land that lawlessness is a crime against the liberty and prosperity of every law-abiding citizen, and is none the less criminal because committed in the name of an irresponsible labor organization; if it shall teach the great body of intelligent citizens that sympathy for law-breakers means direct encouragement to lawlessness; and more than all, if they shall be brought to a realizing sense of the infamous tyranny that is practiced by that small fraction of the working force of the country that is "organized," wherever it has had the opportunity of exhibiting its power, upon the great body of workmen who prefer to exercise their rights, as freemen and sell their labor at their own price. . . .

In contemplating these facts, these questions obtrude themselves: Has the non-union workman no rights that the unionist or amalgamationist is bound to respect? Will the people of this country continue to permit an organized band of ruffians to interfere with the indefensible right of every freeman to earn his living by selling his labor where and to whom he pleases? And, lastly, how long will the employers of labor continue to suffer the insolence and interference of advisory committees, walking delegates, and other creations of trades unionism?

EDITOR'S TABLE

The attitude of the better newspapers of the country with reference to the recent unhappy affair at Homestead has been such as to afford some encouraging

Sources: The Manufacturer and Builder, "The Homestead Affair," August 1892, 185; and *New England Magazine*, "Editor's Table," September 1892, 130–35.

indication that the American people are gradually getting educated upon industrial questions, and getting clearer ideas of relative justice and of some simple matters of right and wrong. The clear headed men of the press have seen plainly, as most men of the pulpit have said . . . that whatever else is to be said about the Homestead strike and its results, the one matter of serious moment and the one great wrong, so great as almost to excuse inattention to all else, was the organization of a private military force by the Carnegie Company, or its manager for the time, a private little army of its own, and the attempt to smuggle this armed force into its fortified works, on its own account, to cope with the disaffected workmen, instead of calling for such protection as was needed upon the constituted authorities of the State. . . .

We have seen exhibitions of "Pinkerton men" in some previous struggles between employers and employees in this country. . . . But we have never had a wholesale exhibition of the character of that which has just been witnessed at Homestead,—and for the credit of the republic it is to be hoped that we shall never have another. . . . No one who is familiar with the government and the social conditions of England or France or Germany can conceive of a great corporation in Liverpool or Lyons or Leipzig, whose property was in any real danger, doing anything but apply to the State for protection and suppression of disorder. . . . The Fort Frick and Pinkerton exhibition which we have just been witnessing at Homestead shows that we are not in advance of the nations of western Europe, but in important respects behind them, in the securities for liberty, equality, and real democracy. It is an exhibition befitting only the feudal middle age. . . . It is insufferable and a thing not to be endured in a democracy, that any men or any companies of men, for whatever purposes incorporated, should have the power of organizing and arming military and police

forces of their own, to act in the settlement of affairs in which they are themselves interested parties, and to shoot men when and how they direct. . . .

The American workingmen are not Anarchists, the men of the American labor unions are not Anarchists,—the sooner all good people take that fact peaceably to heart, the better. . . . Not one brick of the Carnegie property was damaged through all the tumult. Not one of the thousands of striking men, we are authoritatively told, was once found drunk. Of what company of four thousand bankers or railroad magnates, suddenly thrown into a month's idleness at New York or Newport, could as much be said? . . . Let none of us need any second prompting to declare that if any man is indeed piling up millions out of the labor of discontented men, with whom he has driven sharp bargains about wages, and out of the profits is building schools or libraries or hospitals or churches, the title of "Christian philanthropist," which it tickles him this week to wear, shall not outlast the week, but shall give place to the plain and homely label, stuck fatally upon his forehead by the lightning of God—*An unjust man!* Let every one of us hold to strictest account the rich and privileged man.

QUESTIONS

1. What lessons did each magazine draw from the Homestead Lockout? What did Homestead symbolize for each one?
2. According to each magazine, who committed acts of lawlessness?
3. Do these two perspectives share any common ground?
4. What do these contrasting views suggest about the relationship of labor and capital in the Gilded Age?

CHAPTER 18

CITIES, IMMIGRANTS, CULTURE, AND POLITICS, 1877 TO 1900

18.1. COMPETING VISIONS OF THE UNITED STATES AND IMMIGRATION THROUGH POETRY

Jewish American poet Emma Lazarus penned "New Colossus" in 1883 to help raise funds for construction of the Statue of Liberty's pedestal, where the poem was enshrined on a plaque in 1903. Boston nativist Thomas Bailey Aldrich wrote "Unguarded Gates" as a response to "New Colossus" in 1892. "Unguarded Gates" was regularly recited on the floor of Congress by anti-immigration congressmen.

"THE NEW COLOSSUS"

by Emma Lazarus

Not like the brazen giant of Greek fame,
With conquering limbs astride from land to land;
Here at our sea-washed, sunset gates shall stand
A mighty woman with a torch, whose flame
Is the imprisoned lightning, and her name
Mother of Exiles. From her beacon-hand
Glows world-wide welcome; her mild eyes
    command
The air-bridged harbor that twin cities frame.
"Keep, ancient lands, your storied pomp!" cries she
With silent lips. "Give me your tired, your poor,
Your huddled masses yearning to breathe free,
The wretched refuse of your teeming shore.
Send these, the homeless, tempest-tost to me,
I lift my lamp beside the golden door!"

"UNGUARDED GATES"

by Thomas Bailey Aldrich

Wide open and unguarded stand our gates,
Named of the four winds, North, South,
    East and West;
Portals that lead to an enchanted land
Of cities, forests, fields of living gold,
Vast prairies, lordly summits touched with snow,
Majestic rivers sweeping proudly past
The Arab's date-palm and the Norseman's pine—
A realm wherein are fruits of every zone,
Airs of all climes, for lo! throughout the year
The red rose blossoms somewhere—a rich land,
A later Eden planted in the wilds,
With not an inch of earth within its bound
But if a slave's foot press it sets him free.
Here, it is written, Toil shall have its wage,

Source: Emma Lazarus, "The New Colossus," (1883); inscription on the Statue of Liberty, 1903.
Source: Thomas Bailey Aldrich, *Unguarded Gates: and Other Poems* (Boston: Houghton, Mifflin, & Co., 1895), 15-17.

("Unguarded Gates" continued)
And Honor, and the humblest man
Stand level with the highest in the law.
Of such a land have men in dungeons dreamed,
And with the vision brightening in their eyes
Gone smiling to the fagot and the sword.

Wide open and unguarded stand our gates,
And through them presses a wild motley throng—
Men from the Volga and the Tartar steppes,
Featureless figures of the Hoang-Ho,
Malayan, Scythian, Teuton, Kelt, and Slav,
Flying the Old World's poverty and scorn;
These bringing with them unknown gods and rites,
Those, tiger passions, here to stretch their claws.
In street and alley what strange tongues are loud,
Accents of menace alien to our air,
Voices that once the Tower of Babel knew!

O Liberty, white Goddess! Is it well
To leave the gates unguarded? On thy breast

Fold Sorrow's children, soothe the hurts of fate,
Lift the down-trodden, but with hands of steel
Stay those who to thy sacred portals come
To waste the gift of freedom. Have a care
Lest from thy brow clustered stars be torn
And trampled in the dust. For so old
The Thronging Goth and Vandal trampled Rome,
And where the temples and Caesars stood
The Lean wolf unmolested made her lair.

QUESTIONS

1. Compare each poet's ideal vision of the United States.
2. How does each poem describe immigrants?
3. What does Aldrich's poem reveal about the fears of anti-immigrant Americans?
4. What does Lazarus's poem reveal about those who supported unrestricted immigration to the United States?

18.2. VISUAL DOCUMENT: "THE ONLY ONE BARRED OUT," FROM *FRANK LESLIE'S ILLUSTRATED NEWSPAPER* (APRIL 1, 1882)

THE ONLY ONE BARRED OUT.

ENLIGHTENED AMERICAN STATESMAN.—" We must draw the line *somewhere*, you know."

Source: Frank Leslie's illustrated newspaper, vol. 54 (1882 April 1), p. 96./Wikipedia

QUESTIONS

1. What is the cartoonist's position on Chinese exclusion?
2. Discuss the various symbols and the quote that he uses to make his point.
3. How might an anti-Chinese exclusion advocate make an argument against the cartoonist's position and portrayal?

18.3. WIKTORYA AND ANTONI OSINSKI, EXCERPTS FROM LETTERS FROM POLAND TO CHILDREN WHO MIGRATED TO THE UNITED STATES (1902–8)

These letters were dictated by Wiktorya and Antoni Osinski and written by a literate acquaintance to their sons: Jan, who migrated to America first, and Michal (Michalek), who soon followed. The family lived in Poland near the German frontier in an area where residents regularly immigrated to Germany for seasonal work and where immigration to the United States had been occurring for many years.

January 3, 1902

Dear Son,

We thank you nicely for the 10 roubles. You wrote us, dear son, that we might make [from this money] a better Christmas tree and make ourselves merry during the holidays. I should be much merrier if you came here. . . . This money has been of use to us, for we were owing 8 roubles to the carpenter, so your father gave them back at once. He brought 2 roubles home. Of these two we gave 8 zloty for a holy mass, and the rest we took for our Christmas festival. Father says so [to you] "Economize as much as you can so that no one [of your creditors] may drum at your windows when you come back." If our Lord Jesus allows us to get rid of our debts, we shall remember you, for our debts amount to 70 roubles. If God grants us health in this New Year we hope to pay them back, for last year there were only expenses, and no income at all.

Now inform us whether you are near a church, and whether you have already been in it a few times, and how is the divine service celebrated, whether there are sermons and teachings like those in our country. And inform me how do you like America, whether you like it as much as our country. Describe everything, for it is difficult for me [to write you long letters], since I cannot write myself to you. Now I admonish you, dear son, live in the New Year honestly and religiously, for I pray our Lord Jesus for you every day, when going to bed and rising.

May 25, 1902

Dear Son,

You asked me to send you one *gomolka*.[1] When they read it to me, I laughed. It is true that I had none

---

Source: William I. Thomas and Florian Znaniecki, *The Polish Peasant in Europe and America: Monograph of an Immigrant Group* (Boston: Gorham Press, 1918), 1:404–6, 413, 417–18.

1. A small, homemade cheese.

when she left [a cousin going to America], but if she would have taken it, I would have found one. So instead of cheese I send you a godly image—you will have a token—and from every member of the family I send you a small medal. When you receive this image, kiss it, that it may bless you in your work and your health and guard you against a mortal sin. . . . Michal sends you a package of tobacco and Aleksander a package of cigarettes. . . .

You wrote to your father asking, what he would send you. Well, he sends you these words: "Remember always the presence of God. . . ." Now I send you other words: "Work and economize as much as you can." . . .

I can send you nothing more, dear son, except my heart. If I could take it away from my breast and divide it into four parts, as you are four whom our Lord Jesus keep for me still, I would give a part to every one, from love.

July 29, 1903

Dear Son,

You wrote us, dear son, to take a maid-servant, but the worst is that none is to be found; they all go to America. Probably we shall manage alone until you come back. Aleksander can already help me in the heaviest work, he can already reach the sheaves to the cart and then pull them back, and Frania also works as she can. So instead of sending money for the servant, if you have any, send them a little for *okrezne*.[2] Then they will be still more willing to work, and when you come back we shall give you whatever you can. . . . Father was ill for a week; now he has already recovered. . . . I was so grieved, for father lay ill, and Michalek was on the journey—such is my luck, that I am always at work and in grief. . . .

As to Michal, we tried by all means to persuade him not to go, particularly I told him about his journey, how it would be, and that he would be obliged to work heavily. But he always answered that he is ready to work, but he wants to get to America and to be with you. Now I beg you, dear son, if he is in grief, comfort him as much as you can and care for him. You wrote me, dear son, not to grieve about you, but my heart is always in pain that we are not all together or at least all in our country, that we might visit one another.

September 24, 1904

Dear Son,

We are very glad that you are in good health and that you succeed well, so that you even want to take us to America. But for us, your parents, it seems that there is no better America than in this country. Your father says he is too weak and sickens too often. I should be glad to see you, but it is impossible to separate ourselves in our old age. I have also no health; particularly my arms are bad . . . and you wrote that in America one must work hard, and often cannot get work even if he wants it, while here we have always work.

October 29, 1906

Dear Son [Michal],

We received your letter. . . . We are glad that you are in good health for we thought that you all were dead.[3] You had written, dear son, that you would write us something curious, so we waited impatiently thinking that perhaps you were already journeying home. . . . So now when we read this letter of yours we were very much grieved, for we remember you ten times a day and it is very painful to us that you evidently forget us. Dear son, since you did not come, surely we shan't see one another in this world, for this year a penalty was established, that if anybody who belongs to the army went away, his father must pay big money for him, and when he comes back after some years, he must serve his whole time in a disciplinary battalion. . . .

Dear son, you write that you are getting on well enough. Thanks to God for this, but we beg you, we your parents, not to forget about God, then God won't forget about you. It is very hard for us that we cannot see you. More than once we shed bitter tears that we have brought you up and now we cannot be with you. . . . May we at least merit to be in heaven together.

---

2. Harvest festival.
3. Because they had not written home.

April 26, 1908

Dear Children,

We received your letter and the post-notification on Good Friday evening when we came back from the passion. . . .

Dear children, you write that you think about taking Aleksander to America. But we and our work, for whom would it be left? You would all be there and we here. While if he goes to the army for 3 years and God keeps him and brings him happily back, he would help us as he does now. Well, perhaps Frania could remain upon this [farm]; but even so we could see him no more. Moreover, now whole throngs of people are coming back from America . . . and the papers write that it won't be better, but worse.

QUESTIONS

1. What is the tone of these letters? What are the parents' chief concerns for their children who have immigrated to the United States?
2. Based on these letters, what impact did immigration have on the family and other villagers who remained in Poland?
3. Choose one of the letters and, based on your general knowledge of immigrant life in this era, write a response from one of the sons to his parents, addressing their concerns and describing his life in the United States.

18.4. "TENEMENT LIFE IN NEW YORK" (1879)

This article appeared in *Harper's Weekly*, a popular journal with a largely middle-class readership. The article describes living conditions in "Bottle Alley," near Five Points, a notorious neighborhood in lower Manhattan.

It is a time-worn adage that one half the world does not know how the other half lives, and it also might be added, neither does it care. For if it knew the evils of the lower life, it would seek a remedy; if it cared it would not sleep until it had found it and applied it. Especially is it true of large cities that the better classes have hardly begun to suspect what lies beneath the social stratum in which they live, and with all that has been done for the improvement and elevation of the poorer people, the work may be said to have barely been touched, so little comparatively has been accomplished.

Half a million men, women, and children are living in the tenement-houses of New York today, many of them in a manner that would almost disgrace heathendom itself. No brush could paint and no pencil describe with all the vividness of the truth itself the utter wretchedness and misery, the vice and crime, that may be found within a stone's throw of our City Hall, and even within an arm's length of many of our churches. . . .

Many startling facts and figures have been given recently from the pulpit, the platform, and the daily press, in the hope of arousing a public sentiment that may lead to a practical solution of the great problem that is before us.

One of the speakers at the Cooper Institute meeting—Mr. Parker Goodwin—truthfully summed up the whole matter when he said: "These are the homes of the people. The homes! God forgive us for such a prostitution of the blessed word home! As you and I know it, it has no meaning there. . . . As you

Source: "Tenement Life in New York," *Harper's Weekly*, March 22, 1879, 226–27.

and I know it, the home is the resort of peace and joy and love, the centre of the sweetest and tenderest ties, the educator of the young, . . . the source of whatever is noble and manly and truthful in human character, diffusing its gentle influences outward over all society. . . . But are these subterranean caves which a troglodyte of the earliest ages would disdain to enter, are these rayless holes in the wall . . . [,] are these musty and broken garrets which all the rains and winds of the welkin pierce but can not cleanse—are these to be called our homes? Alas! They are the only homes that many of our citizens ever know—where intemperance is nursed, where crime is cradled, where pale-eyed famine and flushed fever lodge, where the instincts of innocent childhood are stifled in the birth, where the modesty of girlhood finds no sheltering veil, where the sobs and sighs of mothers and wives expire in despair, while around them roar the curses of drunken ribaldry and the cries of brutal violence. . . ."

Standing at the entrance, and looking in from the street, no one would ever dream that the tumble-down building in the rear was an abode for human beings. . . .

The cellar is a queer hole. Passing down a flight of stone steps (every one of which is out of joint with its neighbor) and through a dilapidated doorway, the visitor stands in an apartment not much larger than an ordinary hall bedroom, ten by fourteen, with a ceiling so low that he is afraid to keep his hat on lest it brush the dirt from overhead. . . . There are no chairs to sit on, only a few rough boxes. An Italian family of five persons occupied the room until recently, paying $5 a month rent, and taking lodgers—sometimes eight to twelve—at five cents a night. To add to their income they sold sour beer at two cents a pint, or three cents a quart. Dr. Shaffer says in his official report: "Humanity gets no lower than these people are. . . ."

The two upper floors are not quite so bad, but there are sights to be seen in some of the rooms that baffle description. . . . Here five Italians keep bachelors' hall, each one paying his share of the little that is needed to run the concern. One is a carpenter, another a shoemaker, and three are sweepers of the streets. The floor is destitute of carpet, is sunken in one corner, and is covered with grease and dirt. The ceiling and walls are more like those of a smokehouse than of a dwelling. There are no closets or pantries. The cooking utensils hang about the fire-place, the dishes are piled on the table, and the personal effects are crammed into canvas bags that hang from pegs against the walls. None of the vessels used in cooking or serving a meal are ever washed. They are simply emptied or "cleared off," and laid aside for the next meal. The food is gathered principally from the garbage boxes on the streets or from the offal of the markets, and one cooking every week is about all that is done. The sleeping appointments are equally bad. There are no bedsteads. Five filthy-looking mattresses spread on boards supported by carpenters "horses" serve as resting-places. There is no distinction between day and night in the matter of dress. Every man of them goes to bed in the clothes he works in, boots and all, and from one year's end to the other they are never known to wash themselves. . . . They belong to the class who save money, and when they get capital enough together, return to the old country to finish out their days.

QUESTIONS

1. What is the aim of this article?
2. Are the writers more concerned with the plight of tenement dwellers or the threats that tenements pose to larger society?
3. What does this article tell us about middle-class notions of home and family in the Gilded Age?

CHAPTER 19

THE UNITED STATES EXPANDS ITS REACH, 1892 TO 1912

19.1. VISUAL DOCUMENT: "THE ROUGH RIDERS" (*PUCK*, JULY 27, 1898)

Puck, a popular magazine, published this imagined battle scene on its cover several weeks after Theodore Roosevelt led the Rough Riders in their triumphant victory over the Spanish at San Juan Hill.

Source: Everett Collection Inc / Alamy Stock Photo

QUESTIONS

1. How does the cartoonist depict this battle symbolically?

2. How would depictions of Theodore Roosevelt such as this one promote his reputation as an America hero?

19.2. EXCERPTS FROM ANDREW CARNEGIE, "DISTANT POSSESSIONS" (AUGUST 1898), AND ALBERT BEVERIDGE, "THE MARCH OF THE FLAG" (SEPTEMBER 16, 1898)

In August 1898, war with Spain ended and Americans began to debate the question of whether to colonize the Philippines. Two views on this issue are presented here. Steel magnate and outspoken anti-imperialist Andrew Carnegie published the first essay in the *North American Review* in August 1898, shortly after the end of the war. Congressman Albert Beveridge of Indiana delivered the second essay as a speech on September 16, 1898—a month after Carnegie published his anti-imperialist essay—to a Republican meeting in Indianapolis.

DISTANT POSSESSIONS

Twice only have the American people been called upon to decide a question of such vital import as that now before them.

Is the Republic, the apostle of Triumphant Democracy, of the rule of the people, to abandon her political creed and endeavor to establish in other lands the rule of the foreigner over the people, Triumphant Despotism?

Is the Republic to remain one homogeneous whole, one united people, or to become a scattered and disjointed aggregate of widely separated and alien races?

Is she to continue the task of developing her vast continent until it holds a population as great as that of Europe, all Americans, or to abandon that destiny to annex, and to attempt to govern, other far distant parts of the world as outlying possessions, which can never be integral parts of the Republic?

Is she to exchange internal growth and advancement for the development of external possessions which can never be really hers in any fuller sense than India is British, or Cochin-China French? Such is the portentous question of the day. Two equally important questions the American people have decided wisely, and their flag now waves over the greater portion of the English-speaking race; their country is the richest of all countries, first in manufactures, in mining and in commerce (home and foreign), first this year also in exports. But, better than this, the average condition of its people in education and in living is the best. . . . In international affairs her influence grows so fast and foreshadows so much, that one of the foremost statesmen has recently warned Europe that it must combine against her if it is to hold its own in the industrial world. The Republic remains one solid whole, . . . united, impregnable, triumphant; clearly destined to become the foremost power of the world, if she

---

Sources: Andrew Carnegie, "Distant Possessions—The Parting of the Ways," *North American Review*, August 1898, 239–48; and Albert Beveridge, "The March of the Flag," September 16, 1898, http://www.fordham.edu/halsall/mod/1898beveridge.asp.

continues to follow the true path. Such are the fruits of wise judgment in deciding the two great issues of the past, Independence and The Union. . . .

There are two kinds of national possessions, one colonies, the other dependencies. In the former we establish and reproduce our own race. Thus Britain has peopled Canada and Australia with English-speaking people, who have naturally adopted our ideas of self-government. . . .

With "dependencies" it is otherwise. The most grievous burden which Britain has upon her shoulders is that of India, for there it is impossible for our race to grow. The child of English-speaking parents must be removed and reared in Britain. The British Indian official must have long respites in his native land. India means death to our race. . . .

Inasmuch as the territories outside our own continent which our country may be tempted to annex cannot be "colonies," but only "dependencies," we need not dwell particularly upon the advantages or disadvantages of the former. . . .

Some of the organs of manufacturing interests, we observe, favor foreign possessions as necessary or helpful markets for our products. But the exports of the United States this year are greater than those of any other nation in the world. Even Britain's exports are less, and Britain "possesses," it is said, a hundred "colonies" and "dependencies" scattered all over the world. The fact that the United States has none does not prevent her products and manufactures from invading Japan, China, Australia, New Zealand, Canada, and all parts of the world in competition with those of Britain. "Possession" of colonies or dependencies is not necessary for trade reasons. . . .

As long as we remain free from distant possessions, we are impregnable against serious attack; yet, it is true, we have to consider what obligations may fall upon us of an international character requiring us to send our forces to points beyond our own territory. Up to this time we have disclaimed all intention to interfere with affairs beyond our own continent, and only claimed the right to watch over American interests according to the Monroe Doctrine, which is now firmly established. . . . I am no "Little" American, afraid of growth, either in population or territory, provided always that the new territory be American and that it will produce Americans,

and not foreign races bound in time to be false to the Republic in order to be true to themselves. . . .

To reduce it to the concrete, the question is: Shall we attempt to establish ourselves as a power in the Far East and possess the Philippines for glory? The glory we already have, in Dewey's victory. . . . The Philippines have about seven and a half millions of people, composed of races bitterly hostile to one another, alien races, ignorant of our language and institutions. Americans cannot be grown there. . . . But, if we take the Philippines, we shall be forced to govern them as generously as Britain governs her dependencies, which means that they will yield us nothing, and probably be a source of annual expense. Certainly, they will be a grievous drain upon revenue if we consider the enormous army and navy which we shall be forced to maintain upon their account. . . .

The aspirations of a people for independent existence are seldom repressed, nor, according to American ideas hitherto, should they be. . . . Is it possible that the Republic is to be placed in the position of the suppressor of the Philippine struggle for independence? Surely, that is impossible. With what face shall we hang in the school-houses of the Philippines the Declaration of our own Independence, and yet deny independence to them? . . . President McKinley's call for volunteers to fight for Cuban independence against the cruel dominion of Spain meets with prompt response, but who would answer the call of the President of an "imperial" republic for free citizens to fight . . . and slaughter the patriots of some distant dependency which struggles for independence? . . .

Let another phase of the question be carefully weighed. Europe is to-day an armed camp . . . because of fear of aggressive action upon the part of other nations touching outlying "possessions." . . .

It has never been considered the part of wisdom to thrust one's hand into the hornet's nest, and it does seem as if the United States must lose all claim to ordinary prudence and good sense if she enters this arena, and become involved in the intrigues and threats of war which make Europe an armed camp.

If we are to compete with other nations for foreign possession we must have a navy like theirs. . . . While the immense armies of Europe need not be duplicated, yet we shall certainly be too weak unless our army is at least twenty times what it has been—say 500,000 men. Even then we will be powerless as against three of our rivals. . . .

This drain upon the resources of these countries has become a necessity from their respective positions, largely as graspers for foreign possessions. The United States, happily, to-day has no such necessity, her neighbors being powerless against her, since her possessions are concentrated and her power is one solid mass. . . .

From every point of view we are forced to the conclusion that the past policy of the Republic is her true policy for the future; for safety, for peace, for happiness, for progress, for wealth, for power—for all that makes a nation blessed.

THE MARCH OF THE FLAG

It is a noble land that God has given us; a land that can feed and clothe the world; a land whose coastlines would inclose half the countries of Europe; a land set like a sentinel between the two imperial oceans of the globe, a greater England with a nobler destiny.

It is a mighty people that He has planted on this soil; a people sprung from the most masterful blood of history. . . .

It is a glorious history our God has bestowed upon His chosen people; a history heroic with faith in our mission and our future; a history of statesmen who flung the boundaries of the Republic out into unexplored lands and savage wilderness; a history of soldiers who carried the flag across blazing deserts and through the ranks of hostile mountains, even to the gates of sunset; a history of a multiplying people who overran a continent in half a century; a history of prophets who saw the consequences of evils inherited from the past and of martyrs who died to save us from them; a history divinely logical, in the process of whose tremendous reasoning we find ourselves to-day.

Therefore, in this campaign, the question is larger than a party question. It is an American question. It is a world question. Shall the American people continue their march toward the commercial supremacy of the world? Shall free institutions broaden their blessed reign as the children of liberty wax in strength, until the empire of our principles is established over the hearts of all mankind?

Have we no mission to perform, no duty to discharge to our fellow-man? Has God endowed us with gifts beyond our deserts and marked us as the people of His peculiar favor, merely to rot in our own selfishness, as men and nations must, who take cowardice for their companion and self for their deity—as China has, as India has, as Egypt has? . . .

Hawaii is ours; Porto Rico is to be ours; at the prayer of her people Cuba finally will be ours; in the islands of the East, even to the gates of Asia, coaling stations are to be ours at the very least; the flag of a liberal government is to float over the Philippines, and may it be the banner that Taylor unfurled in Texas and Fremont carried to the coast.

The Opposition tells us that we ought not to govern a people without their consent. I answer: The rule of liberty that all just government derives its authority from the consent of the governed, applies only to those who are capable of self-government. We govern the Indians without their consent, we govern our territories without their consent, we govern our children without their consent. How do they know that our government would be without their consent? Would not the people of the Philippines prefer the just, humane, civilizing government of this Republic to the savage, bloody rule of pillage and extortion from which we have rescued them?

They ask us how we shall govern these new possessions. I answer: Out of local conditions and the necessities of the case methods of government will grow. If England can govern foreign lands, so can America. If Germany can govern foreign lands, so can America. If they can supervise protectorates, so can America. Why is it more difficult to administer Hawaii than New Mexico or California? Both had a savage and an alien population; both were more remote from the seat of government when they came under our dominion than the Philippines are to-day. . . .

There are so many real things to be done—canals to be dug, railways to be laid, forests to be felled, cities to be builded, fields to be tilled, markets to be won, ships to be launched, peoples to be saved, civilization to be proclaimed and the flag of liberty flung to the eager air of every sea. Is this an hour to waste upon triflers with nature's laws? Is this a season to give our destiny over to word-mongers and prosperity wreckers? No! It is an hour to remember our duty to our homes. It is a moment to realize the opportunities fate has opened to us. And so it is an hour for us to stand by the Government.

Wonderfully has God guided us. Yonder at Bunker Hill and Yorktown His Providence was above us. At New Orleans and on ensanguined seas His hand sustained us. Abraham Lincoln was His minister and His was the altar of freedom the Nation's soldiers set up on a hundred battle-fields. His power directed Dewey in the East and delivered the Spanish fleet into our hands, as He delivered the elder Armada into the hands of our English sires two centuries ago. The American people can not use a dishonest medium of exchange; it is ours to set the world its example of right and honor. We can not fly from our world duties; it is ours to execute the purpose of a fate that has driven us to be greater than our small intentions. We can not retreat from any soil where Providence has unfurled our banner; it is ours to save that soil for liberty and civilization.

QUESTIONS

1. Why does Carnegie believe that the United States should refrain from colonizing the Philippines, and why does Beveridge think the United States should make the Philippines a colony?

2. How do both Carnegie and Beveridge use history to make their claims?

3. Who do you think makes the most convincing case overall? Why?

4. How do Carnegie and Beveridge define *American*? What role does race play in the arguments of each man?

19.3. VISUAL DOCUMENT: UNTITLED CLIFFORD BERRYMAN CARTOON (1899)

This cartoon by Clifford Berryman appeared in the *Washington Post* on February 4, 1899, as U.S. military forces attempted to subdue the Filipino independence movement led by Emilio Aguinaldo.

QUESTIONS

1. What title would you give this untitled cartoon?
2. Is the cartoonist for or against Filipino independence?
3. What images does he use to make his point of view clear?

Source: Berryman, Clifford. Washington Post, February 4, 1899. /The U.S. National Archives

19.4. RICHMOND PLANET AND WISCONSIN WEEKLY ADVOCATE, EXCERPTS FROM LETTERS FROM AFRICAN AMERICAN SOLDIERS IN THE PHILIPPINES (1899–1900)

Black soldiers serving in the Philippines to put down the insurgency against the United States sent letters to African American newspapers relating their experiences on the islands. Some disheartened soldiers found that the color line extended far beyond the boundaries of the United States, while others saw action in the Philippines as a chance to prove their patriotism and their equality. The first and third letters printed here were published in the *Richmond Planet* on December 30, 1899, and December 22, 1900, respectively. The second letter was published in the Milwaukee newspaper *Wisconsin Weekly Advocate* on May 17, 1900.

Dear Mr. Editor:

We received copies of the *Planet* sent to us at this point. You can imagine how much we appreciated them when we had not seen a paper of any kind for weeks, and as for an Afro-American paper, I can not remember when I last laid eyes on one. . . .

The whites have begun to establish their diabolical race hatred in all its home rancor in Manila, even endeavoring to propagate the phobia among the Spaniards and Filipinos so as to be sure of the foundation of their supremacy when the civil rule that must necessarily follow the present military regime, is established.

I felt it worth the while to check the Filipino as to his knowledge and view of the American colored man that we might know our position intelligently. What follows is a condensed account of the results. The questions were put to the intelligent, well-educated Filipinos. . . .

QUES. Do the Filipinos hold a different feeling toward the colored American from that of the white?

ANS. "Before American occupation of the islands and before colored troops came to the Philippines, Filipinos knew little if anything of the colored people of America. . . . All were simply Americans to us. This view was held up to the time of the arrival of the colored regiments in Manila, when the white troops, seeing your acceptance on a social plane by the Filipino and Spaniard was equal to, if not better than theirs, . . . began to tell us of the inferiority of the American blacks—of your brutal natures, your cannibal tendencies—how you would rape our senioritas, etc. Of course, at first we were a little shy of you, after being told of the difference between you and them; but we studied you, as results have shown. Between you and him, we look upon you as the angel and him as the devil.

"Of course, you are both Americans, and conditions between us are constrained, and neither can be our friends in the sense of friendship, but the affinity of complexion between you and me tells, and you exercise your duty so much more kindly and manly in dealing with us. We can not help but appreciate the differences between you and the whites."

Interview of Senor Tordorica Santos, a Filipino physician. By the difference in "dealing with us" expressed is meant that the colored soldiers do not push them off the streets, spit at them, call them damned "niggers," abuse them in all manner of ways, and

Source: Willard B. Gatewood Jr., *Smoked Yankees and the Struggle for Empire: Letters from Negro Soldiers, 1898–1902* (Fayetteville: University of Arkansas Press, 1987), 251–55, 279–81, 284–85.

connect race hatred with duty, for the colored soldiers has none such for them.

The future of the Filipino, I fear, is that of the Negro in the South. Matters are almost to that condition now. No one (white) has any scruples as regards respecting the rights of a Filipino. He is kicked and cuffed at will and he dare not remonstrate. . . .

Yours truly,
John W. Galloway
Sgt. Major,
24th U.S. Infantry

Editor, New York Age

• • •

I have mingled freely with the natives and have had talks with American colored men here in business and who have lived here for years, in order to learn of them the cause of their (Filipino) dissatisfaction and the reason for this insurrection, and I must confess they have a just grievance. All this never would have occurred if the army of occupation would have treated them as people. The Spaniards, even if their laws were hard, were polite and treated them with consideration; but the Americans, as soon as they saw that the native troops were desirous of sharing in the glories as well as the hardships of the hard-won battles with the Americans, began to apply home treatment for colored peoples: cursed them as damned niggers, steal [from] and ravish them, rob them on the street of their small change, take from the fruit vendors whatever suited their fancy, and kick the poor unfortunate if he complained, desecrate their church property, and after fighting began, looted everything in sight, burning, robbing the graves.

This may seem a little tall—but I have seen with my own eyes carcasses lying bare in the boiling sun, the results of raids on receptacles for the dead in search of diamonds. The [white] troops, thinking we would be proud to emulate their conduct, have made bold of telling their exploits to us. One fellow, member of the 13th Minnesota, told me how some fellows he knew had cut off a native woman's arm in order to get a fine inlaid bracelet. On upbraiding some fellows one

morning, whom I met while out for a walk (I think they belong to a Nebraska or Minnesota regiment, and they were stationed on the Malabon road) for the conduct of the American troops toward the natives and especially as to raiding, etc., the reply was: "Do you think we could stay over here and fight these damn niggers without making it pay all it's worth? The government only pays us $13 per month: that's starvation wages. White men can't stand it." Meaning they could not live on such small pay. In saying this they never dreamed that Negro soldiers would never countenance such conduct. They talked with impunity of "niggers" to our soldiers, never once thinking that they were talking to home "niggers" and should they be brought to remember that at home this is the same vile epithet they hurl at us, they beg pardon and make some effeminate excuse about what the Filipino is called.

I want to say right here that if it were not for the sake of the 10,000,000 black people in the United States, God alone knows on which side of the subject I would be. And for the sake of the black men who carry arms for them as their representatives, ask them to not forget the present administration at the next election. Party be damned! We don't want these islands, not in the way we are to get them, and for Heaven's sake, put the party [Democratic] in power that pledged itself against this highway robbery. Expansion is too clean a name for it.

[Unsigned]

• • •

Sir:

I have the honor to address you as to the present situation in the Philippines. Two battalions of the 25th Infantry, colored, arrived in Manila Bay on July 31st, 1899. . . . Since our landing on the Island of Luzon we have executed some of as hard and effective work as any other regiment in the Philippines, also made some of the more important captures of the campaign. . . .

Wherever we have been stationed on the islands we have made friends with the natives and they always express regret when we are ordered from amongst them, especially if we have been stationed near them for any length of time.

Our officers and men always make it a rule wherever we are stationed to treat the natives with civility and we have always complied with this rule. . . .

We treat them with due consideration, insurgent prisoners as well as peaceable natives; but whenever they show fight, they are greeted with a warm reception and they soon learn to their discontent what kind of fighting material, the seemingly peaceable black fighters of Uncle Sam's regular army are made out of.

We have been stationed in Zambales Province longer than in any other one place on the Island. We were the first U.S. soldiers to enter the province where we were met with strong resistance, but the Filipinos never once had the nerve to stand their ground when they were charged upon by the dusky fighters. They never have once scored a victory over the 25th Infantry. . . .

We were jubilant over the prospects of going to China a few weeks ago, but . . . our wise Excellency, the President, has restored peace, which he always does whenever his good and wise judgment is called into play. The 25th would like to have had China added to her list, but we will be contented with our past accomplishments; but whenever duty calls us we will not be weighed and found wanting. Our courage has won us fame; our moral principles and kindness have won us friends; our good workmanship and how to deal with the enemy have won us fear; our good discipline has won us praise from our superiors. . . .

I have read a good many accounts, by discharged volunteers and regulars through the American newspapers, of depredations committed upon Filipinos by our men in the field, which reports are false. . . . The prisoners as well as the peaceable [natives] are treated with great consideration. Our officers take great pride in protecting [the natives]. . . .

If a person were to search the roots of these reports they could easily see where they originate. Some men came into the army for pleasure and some for adventure, but when they enlist and are presented their field equipment and commence camp life, their expectation of feather mattresses . . . ham and eggs, quail on toast and other such delicacies are not realized, they commence to cry to go home; they generally turn [out] to be chronic kickers and newspaper correspondents.

It seems as if they expect to campaign in a Pullman Palace Car. The American Army is better off without such men. . . . They should be corralled up and fed on beeftea and chicken broth until they can be given back to their parents. . . .

> *Respectfully yours,*
> *James Booker*
> *Co. H, 25th Infantry*

QUESTIONS

1. Based on these letters, what conclusions can you draw about the experiences of black soldiers in the Philippines?

2. What evidence suggests that these black soldiers experienced the war differently than white soldiers? What evidence suggests that their wartime experience was the same?

3. Two letters remark on violence perpetrated on Filipinos by American soldiers, whereas one letter claims these events never happened. What might account for this difference? What additional sources would you seek out to substantiate how soldiers treated Filipinos during the war?

CHAPTER 20

AN AGE OF PROGRESSIVE REFORM, 1890 TO 1920

20.1. CONGRESSMAN GEORGE H. WHITE, EXCERPTS FROM FAREWELL ADDRESS TO CONGRESS (JANUARY 29, 1901)

With the rise of segregation, disfranchisement, and a vicious white supremacy campaign in his home state of North Carolina, Congressman George H. White, the only black congressman at the turn of the twentieth century, chose not to run for a third term, seeing his chances of being reelected as hopeless. He gave his last speech on the floor of Congress on January 29, 1901. It would be another twenty-eight years before another black representative sat in Congress.

I want to enter a plea for the colored man, the colored woman, the colored boy, and the colored girl of this country. I would not thus digress from the question at issue and detain the House in a discussion of the interests of this particular people at this time but for the constant and the persistent efforts of certain gentlemen upon this floor to mold and rivet public sentiment against us as a people and to lose no opportunity to hold up the unfortunate few who commit crimes and depredations and lead lives of infamy and shame, as other races do, as fair specimens of representatives of the entire colored race. . . .

In the catalogue of members of Congress in this House perhaps none have been more persistent in their determination to bring the black man into disrepute and, with a labored effort, to show that he was unworthy of the right of citizenship than my colleague from North Carolina, Mr. Kitchin. During the first session of this Congress . . . he labored long and hard to show that the white race was at all times and under all circumstances superior to the Negro by inheritance if not otherwise, and . . . that an illiterate Negro was unfit to participate in making the laws of a sovereign state and the administration and execution of them; but an illiterate white man living by his side, with no more or perhaps not as much property, with no more exalted character, no higher thoughts of civilization, no more knowledge of the handicraft of government, had by birth, because he was white, inherited some peculiar qualification. . . .

Source: George H. White, speech addressed to the U.S. House of Representatives, January 29, 1901, 56th Cong., 2d Sess., *Congressional Record* 34, pt. 2:1635–38.

In the town where this young gentleman was born, at the general election last August . . . , Scotland Neck had a registered white vote of 395, most of whom of course were Democrats, and a registered colored vote of 534, virtually if not all of whom were Republicans, and so voted. When the count was announced, however, there were 831 Democrats to 75 Republicans; but in the town of Halifax, same county, the result was much more pronounced.

In that town the registered Republican vote was 345, and the total registered vote of the township was 539, but when the count was announced it stood 990 Democrats to 41 Republicans, or 492 more Democratic votes counted than were registered votes in the township. Comment here is unnecessary. . . .

It would be unfair, however, for me to leave the inference upon the minds of those who hear me that all of the white people of the State of North Carolina hold views with Mr. Kitchin and think as he does. Thank God there are many noble exceptions to the example he sets, that, too, in the Democratic party; men who have never been afraid that one uneducated, poor, depressed Negro could put to flight and chase into degradation two educated, wealthy, thrifty white men. There never has been, nor ever will be, any Negro domination in that State, and no one knows it any better than the Democratic party. It is a convenient howl, however, often resorted to in order to consummate a diabolical purpose by scaring the weak and gullible whites into support of measures and men suitable to the demagogue. . . .

I trust I will be pardoned for making a passing reference to one more gentleman—Mr. Wilson of South Carolina—who, in the early part of this month, made a speech, some parts of which did great credit to him. . . . But his purpose was incomplete until he dragged in the reconstruction days and held up to scorn and ridicule the few ignorant, gullible, and perhaps purchasable Negroes who served in the State legislature of South Carolina over thirty years ago. . . . These few ignorant men who chanced at that time to hold office are given as a reason why the black man should not be permitted to participate in the affairs of the Government which he is forced to pay taxes to support. . . .

If the gentleman to whom I have referred will pardon me, I would like to advance the statement that the musty records of 1868 . . . as to what the Negro was thirty-two years ago, is not a proper standard by which the Negro living on the threshold of the twentieth century should be measured. Since that time we have reduced the illiteracy of the race at least 45 percent. We have written and published nearly 500 books. We have nearly 300 newspapers, 3 of which are dailies. We have now in practice over 2,000 lawyers, and a corresponding number of doctors. We have accumulated over $12,000,000 worth of school property and about $40,000,000 worth of church property. We have about 140,000 farms and homes, valued in the neighborhood of $750,000,000, and personal property valued about $170,000,000. We have raised about $11,000,000 for educational purposes, and the property per-capita for every colored man, woman and child in the United States is estimated at $75.

We are operating successfully several banks, commercial enterprises among our people in the South land, including one silk mill and one cotton factory. We have 32,000 teachers in the schools of the country; we have built, with the aid of our friends, about 20,000 churches, and support 7 colleges, 17 academies, 50 high schools, 5 law schools, 5 medical schools, and 25 theological seminaries. We have over 600,000 acres of land in the South alone. The cotton produced, mainly by black labor, has increased from 4,669,770 bales in 1860 to 11,235,000 in 1899. All this we have done under the most adverse circumstances.

We have done it in the face of lynching, burning at the stake, with the humiliation of "Jim Crow" cars, the disfranchisement of our male citizens, slander and degradation of our women, with the factories closed against us, no Negro permitted to be conductor on the railway cars . . . no Negro permitted to run as engineer on a locomotive, most of the mines closed against us. Labor unions—carpenters, painters, brick masons, machinists, hackmen and those supplying nearly every conceivable avocation for livelihood—have banded themselves together to better their condition, but, with few exceptions, the black face has been left out. The Negroes are seldom employed in our mercantile stores. . . .

With all these odds against us, we are forging our way ahead, slowly, perhaps, but surely. You may tie us and then taunt us for lack of bravery, but one day we will break the bonds. You may use our labor for two and a half centuries and then taunt us for our poverty, but let me remind you we will not always remain poor. You may withhold even the knowledge of how to read God's word and . . . then taunt us for our ignorance, but we would remind you that there is plenty of room at the top, and we are climbing. . . .

Now Mr. Chairman, before concluding my remarks I want to submit a brief recipe for the solution of the so-called American negro problem. He asks no special favors, but simply demands that he be given the same chance for existence, for earning a livelihood, for raising himself in the scales of manhood and womanhood, that are accorded to kindred nationalities. Treat him as a man; go into his home and learn his social conditions; learn of his cares, his troubles, and his hopes for the future; gain his confidence; open the doors of industry to him; let the word "negro," "colored," and "black" be stricken from all the organizations enumerated in the federation of labor. Help him to overcome his weaknesses, punish the crime-committing class by the courts of the land, measure the standard of the race by its best material, cease to mold prejudicial and unjust public sentiment against him, and my word for it, he will learn to support, hold up the hands of, and join in with that political party,

that institution, whether secular or religious, in every community where he lives, which is destined to do the greatest good for the greatest number. Obliterate race hatred, party prejudice, and help us to achieve nobler ends, greater results and become satisfactory citizens to our brother in white.

This, Mr. Chairman, is perhaps the negroes' temporary farewell to the American Congress; but let me say, Phoenix-like he will rise up some day and come again. . . .

The only apology I have to make for the earnestness with which I have spoken is that I am pleading for the life, the liberty, the future happiness, and manhood suffrage for one-eighth of the entire population of the United States.

QUESTIONS

1. According to Congressman White, how did the Democrats manage to push blacks out of office?
2. How, according to the speech, did white Democrats mischaracterize history to regain power in North Carolina?
3. How does Congressman White use history to defend the right of black Americans to vote and hold office?

Source: Norman Rockwell Museum, https://www.illustrationhistory.org/illustrations/womens-suffrage-poster

QUESTIONS

1. Compare how both pro- and antisuffrage supporters used children and the home to justify their positions.
2. How did both pro- and antisuffragists view the place of women in U.S. society?
3. Did each side share some common assumptions? How did they differ?

Source: The Miriam and Ira D. Wallach Division of Art, Prints and Photographs: Art & Architecture Collection, The New York Public Library. "The home or street corner for woman? Vote no on woman suffrage." The New York Public Library Digital Collections. 1978.

20.3. EMILY P. BISSELL, "[A] TALK TO WOMEN ON THE SUFFRAGE QUESTION" (1909)

Emily Bissell, a social worker and activist, was a well-known antisuffragist. She testified before the U.S. Senate Committee on Woman Suffrage in 1900, arguing that women had no business in politics. This talk was originally published in 1909 by the New York State Association Opposed to Woman Suffrage.

There are three points of view from which every woman today ought to consider herself—as an individual, as a member of a family, as a member of the state. Every woman stands in those three relations to American life. . . .

The proposal that women should vote affects each one of these three relations deeply. . . . There are grave objections to woman suffrage on all these three counts. Sixty years of argument and of effort on the part of the suffragists have not in the least changed these arguments, because they rest on the great fundamental facts of human nature and of human government. The suffrage is "a reform against nature" and such reforms are worse than valueless.

Let us take these three points of view singly. Why, in the first place, is the vote a mistake for women as individuals? . . . The claims upon a woman's time, in this twentieth century, are greater than ever before. Woman, in her progress, has taken up many important things to deal with, and has already overloaded herself beyond her strength. . . . Most of the self-supporting women of my acquaintance do not want the ballot. They have no time to think about it. Most of the wives and mothers I know do not want to vote. They are too busy with other burdens. Most of the women of affairs I know do not want to vote. They are doing public work without it better than they could do with it, and consider it a burden, not a benefit. The ballot is a duty, a responsibility; and most intelligent, active women to-day believe that it is a man's duty and responsibility, and that they are not called to take it up in addition to their own share. . . . The suffragists cannot get the vote without forcing it on all the rest of womankind in America; for America means unrestricted manhood suffrage, and an equal suffrage law would mean unrestricted womanhood suffrage, from the college girl to the immigrant woman who cannot read and the negro woman in the cotton-field, and from the leader of society down to the drunken woman in the police court. . . .

. . . The American home is the foundation of American strength and progress. And in the American home woman has her place and her own duty to family. . . .

The family demands from a woman her very best. Her highest interests, and her unceasing care, must be in home life, if her home is to be what it ought to be. Here is where the vote for woman comes in as a disturbing factor. The vote is part of man's work. Ballot-box, cartridge box, jury box, sentry box, all go together in his part of life. Woman cannot step in and take the responsibilities and duties of voting without assuming his place very largely. . . .

The individualism of woman, in these modern days, is a threat to the family. There is one divorce in America nowadays to every dozen marriages. There are thousands of young women who crowd into the factory or mill or office in preference to home duties. There is an impatience of ties and responsibilities, a restlessness, a fever for "living one's own life," that is unpleasantly noticeable. The desire for the vote is part of this restlessness, this grasping for power that shall have no responsibility except to drop a paper into a ballot box, this ignorant desire to do "the work of the world" instead of one's own appointed work. If women had conquered their own part of life perfectly, one might wish to see them thus leave it and go forth to set the world to rights. But on the contrary, never were domestic conditions so badly

Source: Edith M. Phelps ed., *Selected Articles on Woman Suffrage*, 3rd. and rev. ed. (White Plains and New York: H.W. Wilson Co., 1916), 145–151.

attended to. Until woman settles the servant question, how can she ask to run the government?

This brings us to the third point, which is, the effect on the state of a vote for women. . . .

One thing sure—the woman's vote would be an indifferent one. The majority of women do not want to vote—even the suffragists acknowledge that. Therefore, if given the vote they would not be eager voters. . . . The greatest trouble in politics to-day is the indifferent vote among men. Equal suffrage would add a larger indifferent vote among women.

Then there is the corrupt vote to-day. Among men it is bad enough. But among women it would be much worse. . . . Unrestricted suffrage must reckon with all kinds of women, you see—and the unscrupulous woman will use her vote for what it is worth and for corrupt ends.

Today, without the vote, the women who are intelligent and interested in public affairs use their ability and influence for good measures. And the indifferent woman does not matter. The unscrupulous woman has no vote, we get the best, and bar out the rest. The state gets all the benefit of its best women, and none of the danger from its worst women. . . .

Where would the state be then—with an indifferent vote, a corrupt vote, and a helpless, unorganized vote, loaded on to its present political difficulties? Where would the state be with a doubled negro vote in the Black Belt? Where would New York and Chicago be with a doubled immigrant vote?

QUESTIONS

1. What are the author's main reasons for opposing votes for women?
2. How would a suffragist respond to the author's main points?
3. Based on this reading, what role did race, class, and anti-immigrant sentiment play in the antisuffrage movement?

20.4. EUGENE V. DEBS, SPEECH IN CANTON, OHIO (1918)

After making this speech on June 16, 2018, American Socialist Party leader Eugene V. Debs was immediately arrested by the federal government for violating the Espionage Act (1917) and Sedition Act (1918) passed by Congress during World War I, severely limiting free speech and making it a federal offense to obstruct or speak against the government in any way deemed treasonous. Slapped with a ten-year jail sentence, Debs nevertheless ran for president from prison in 1920. His arrest was only one of many during and after the war that decimated the Socialist Party in the United States.

Comrades, friends and fellow-workers, for this very cordial greeting, this very hearty reception, I thank you all with the fullest appreciation of your interest in and your devotion to the cause for which I am to speak to you this afternoon.

To speak for labor; to plead the cause of the men and women and children who toil; to serve the working class, has always been to me a high privilege; a duty of love.

I have just returned from a visit over yonder, where three of our most loyal comrades are paying the penalty for their devotion to the cause of the working class. They have come to realize, as many of us have, that it is extremely dangerous to exercise the constitutional right of free speech in a country fighting to make democracy safe in the world.

I realize that, in speaking to you this afternoon, there are certain limitations placed upon the right of

Source: The Call, June 1918.

free speech. I must be exceedingly careful, prudent, as to what I say, and even more careful and prudent as to how I say it. I may not be able to say all I think; but I am not going to say anything that I do not think. I would rather a thousand times be a free soul in jail than to be a sycophant and coward in the streets. They may put those boys in jail—and some of the rest of us in jail—but they can not put the Socialist movement in jail. . . .

Wars throughout history have been waged for conquest and plunder. In the Middle Ages when the feudal lords who inhabited the castles whose towers may still be seen along the Rhine concluded to enlarge their domains, to increase their power, their prestige and their wealth they declared war upon one another. But they themselves did not go to war any more than the modern feudal lords, the barons of Wall Street go to war. The feudal barons of the Middle Ages, the economic predecessors of the capitalists of our day, declared all wars. And their miserable serfs fought all the battles. The poor, ignorant serfs had been taught to revere their masters; to believe that when their masters declared war upon one another, it was their patriotic duty to fall upon one another and to cut one another's throats for the profit and glory of the lords and barons who held them in contempt. And that is war in a nutshell. The master class has always declared the wars; the subject class has always fought the battles. The master class has had all to gain and nothing to lose, while the subject class has had nothing to gain and all to lose—especially their lives.

They have always taught and trained you to believe it to be your patriotic duty to go to war and to have yourselves slaughtered at their command. But in all the history of the world you, the people, have never had a voice in declaring war, and strange as it certainly appears, no war by any nation in any age has ever been declared by the people.

And here let me emphasize the fact—and it cannot be repeated too often—that the working class who fight all the battles, the working class who make the supreme sacrifices, the working class who freely shed their blood and furnish the corpses, have never yet had

a voice in either declaring war or making peace. It is the ruling class that invariably does both. They alone declare war and they alone make peace.

Yours not to reason why; Yours but to do and die.

That is their motto and we object on the part of the awakening workers of this nation.

If war is right let it be declared by the people. You who have your lives to lose, you certainly above all others have the right to decide the momentous issue of war or peace. . . .

It is the minorities who have made the history of this world. It is the few who have had the courage to take their places at the front; who have been true enough to themselves to speak the truth that was in them; who have dared oppose the established order of things; who have espoused the cause of the suffering, struggling poor; who have upheld without regard to personal consequences the cause of freedom and righteousness. . . .

Do you wish to hasten the day of victory? Join the Socialist Party! Don't wait for the morrow. Join now! Enroll your name without fear and take your place where you belong. . . .

You need at this time especially to know that you are fit for something better than slavery and cannon fodder. You need to know that you were not created to work and produce and impoverish yourself to enrich an idle exploiter. You need to know that you have a mind to improve, a soul to develop, and a manhood to sustain. . . .

Do not worry over the charge of treason to your masters, but be concerned about the treason that involves yourselves. Be true to yourself and you cannot be a traitor to any good cause on earth.

Yes, in good time we are going to sweep into power in this nation and throughout the world. We are going to destroy all enslaving and degrading capitalist institutions and re-create them as free and humanizing institutions. The world is daily changing before our eyes. The sun of capitalism is setting; the sun of socialism is rising. It is our duty to build the new nation and the free republic. We need industrial and social builders. We Socialists are the builders of the beautiful world that is to be. We are all pledged to do our part. We are inviting—aye challenging you this afternoon in the name of your own manhood and womanhood to join us and do your part.

In due time the hour will strike and this great cause triumphant—the greatest in history—will proclaim the emancipation of the working class and the brotherhood of all mankind.

QUESTIONS

1. How does Debs characterize the Great War waging in Europe? According to Debs, what is the war about?
2. Why was Debs's speech considered so threatening by the federal government?
3. Do you think the government has the right to limit speech in wartime? Why? Why not?

CHAPTER 21

AMERICA AND THE GREAT WAR, 1914 TO 1920

21.1. VISUAL DOCUMENTS: PROPAGANDA POSTERS (1914–18)

Propaganda posters issued by U.S. government agencies and voluntary organizations reached and informed millions of Americans during World War I. These posters urged men to join the armed forces, women to take war production jobs, citizens to buy war bonds, people on the home front to send cigarettes to soldiers, and the public to support the proposed League of Nations.

Source: James Montgomery Flagg, Send Smokes to Sammy! Our Boys in France Tobacco Fund (1918) © Swim Ink 2, LLC/CORBIS
Source: Howard Chandler Christy, Clear The Way!! Buy Bonds, Fourth Liberty Loan (c. 1918) © CORBIS.

QUESTIONS

1. How did this poster art simplify complex questions?

2. To what emotions did propaganda posters appeal?

3. How did suffragists link U.S. goals in World War I to domestic political reform? Why did they call President Wilson a hypocrite?

21.2. COMMITTEE ON PUBLIC INFORMATION, "GENERAL SUGGESTIONS TO SPEAKERS" (MAY 22, 1917) AND "SPEECH BY A FOUR MINUTE MAN" (OCTOBER 8, 1917)

The government's Committee on Public Information organized prowar educational activities at home and abroad during World War I. The committee recruited seventy-five thousand amateur orators called "Four Minute Men" to give brief speeches in movie theaters, schools, churches, and union halls in English and dozens of other languages ranging from Yiddish and Italian to Sioux. These speeches warned of enemy efforts to subvert the war effort and the importance of national unity.

Source: Everett Collection Inc / Alamy Stock Photo
Sources: Committee on Public Information, *Four Minute Men Bulletin* 1, May 22, 1917; and Committee on Public Information, *Four Minute Men Bulletin* 17, October 8, 1917.

"GENERAL SUGGESTIONS TO SPEAKERS"

The speech must not be longer than four minutes, which means there is no time for a single wasted word.

Speakers should go over their speech time and time again until the ideas are firmly fixed in their mind and can not be forgotten. This does not mean that the speech needs to be written out and committed,[1] although most speakers, especially when limited in time, do best to commit.

Divide your speech carefully into certain divisions, say 15 seconds for final appeal; 45 seconds to describe the bond; 15 seconds for opening words, etc., etc. Any plan is better than none, and it can be amended every day in the light of experience.

There never was a speech yet that couldn't be improved. Never be satisfied with success. Aim to be more successful, and still more successful. So keep your eyes open. Read all the papers every day, to find a new slogan, or a new phraseology, or a new idea to replace something you have in your speech. For instance, the editorial page of the *Chicago Herald* of May 19 is crammed full of good ideas and phrases. Most of the article is a little above the average audience, but if the ideas are good, you should plan carefully to bring them into the experience of your auditors. There is one sentence which says, "No country was ever saved by the other fellow; it must be done by you, by a hundred million yous, or it will not be done at all." Or again, Secretary McAdoo says, "Every dollar invested in the Liberty Loan is a real blow for liberty, a blow against the militaristic system which would strangle the freedom of the world," and so on. Both the *Tribune* and the *Examiner*, besides the *Herald*, contain President Wilson's address to the nation in connection with the draft registration. The latter part is very suggestive and can be used effectively. Try slogans like "Earn the right to say, I helped to win the war," and "This is a Loyalty Bond as well as a Liberty Bond," or "A cause that is worth living for is worth dying for, and a cause that is worth dying for is worth fighting for." Conceive of your speech as a mosaic made up of five or six hundred words, each one of which has its function.

If you come across a new slogan, or a new argument, or a new story, or a new illustration, don't fail to send it to the Committee. We need your help to make the Four-Minute Men the mightiest force for arousing patriotism in the United States.

"SPEECH BY A FOUR MINUTE MAN"

Ladies and Gentlemen:

I have just received the information that there is a German spy among us—a German spy watching *us*.

He is around, here somewhere, reporting upon you and me—sending reports about us to Berlin and telling the Germans just what we are doing with the Liberty Loan. From every section of the country these spies have been getting reports over to Potsdam—not general reports but details—where the loan is going well and where its success seems weak, and what people are saying in each community.

For the German Government is worried about our great loan. Those Junkers fear its effect upon the German *morale*. They're raising a loan this month, too.

If the American people lend their billions now, one and all with a hip-hip-hurrah, it means that America is united and strong. While, if we lend our money half-heartedly, America seems weak and autocracy remains strong.

Money means everything now; it means quicker victory and therefore less bloodshed. We are *in* the war, and now Americans can have but *one* opinion, only *one* wish in the Liberty Loan.

Well, I hope these spies are getting their messages straight, letting Potsdam know that America is *hurling back* to the autocrats these answers:

For treachery here, attempted treachery in Mexico, treachery everywhere—*one billion.*

For murder of American women and children—*one billion more.*

For broken faith and promise to murder more Americans—*billions and billions more.*

And then we will add:

---

1. Memorized.

In the world fight for Liberty, our share—*billions and billions and billions and endless billions.*

Do not let the German spy hear and report that *you* are a slacker.

21.3. THEODORE ROOSEVELT, "THE HUN WITHIN OUR GATES" (1917)

Former President Theodore Roosevelt criticized President Woodrow Wilson's reluctance to enter World War I. Once the United States did so, in April 1917, Roosevelt launched a campaign against all Americans whom he deemed less enthusiastic war supporters than himself. In this article he published in 1917, Roosevelt denounced many politicians, ethnic Americans, labor activists, pacifists, and others whom he accused of being German agents.

The Hun within our gates is the worst of the foes of our own household, whether he is the paid or the unpaid agent of Germany. Whether he is pro-German or poses as a pacifist, or a peace-at-any-price man, matters little. He is the enemy of the United States. Senators and Congressmen like Messrs. Stone, La Follette and Maclemore belong in Germany and it is a pity they cannot be sent there. . . . Such men are among the worst of the foes of our own household; and so are the sham philanthropists and sinister agitators and the wealthy creatures without patriotism who support and abet them. Our Government has seemed afraid to grapple with these people. It is permitting thousands of allies of Berlin to sow the seeds of treason and sedition in this country. The I.W.W. boasts its defiance of all law, and many of its members exultingly proclaim that in their war against industry in the United States they are endeavoring to give the Government so much to do that it will have no troops to spare for Europe. Every district where the I.W.W. starts rioting should be placed under martial law, and cleaned up by military methods. The German-language papers carry on a consistent campaign in favor of Germany against England. They should be put out of existence for the period of this war. The Hearst papers, more ably edited than the German sheets, play the Kaiser's game in a similar way. When they keep within the law they should at least be made to feel the scorn felt for them by every honest American. Wherever any editor can be shown to be purveying treason in violation of law he should be jailed until the conflict is over. Every disloyal German-born citizen should have his naturalization papers recalled and should be interned during the term of the war. Action of this kind is especially necessary in order to pick out the disloyal but vociferous minority of citizens of German descent from the vast but silent majority of entirely loyal citizens of German descent who otherwise will suffer from a public anger that will condemn all alike. Every disloyal native-born American should be disfranchised and interned. It is time to strike our enemies at home heavily and quickly. Every copperhead in this country is an enemy to the Government, to the people, to the army and to the flag, and should be treated as such.

This pro-German, anti-American propaganda has been carried on for years prior to the war, and its treasonable activities are performed systematically to-day. . . . These men support and direct the pro-German societies. They incite disloyal activities among the Russian Jews. They finance the small groups of Irish-Americans whose hatred for England makes them traitors to the United

Source: Theodore Roosevelt, *The Foes of Our Own Household* (New York: George H. Doran, 1917), 293–95.

States. They foment seditious operations among the German-American socialists and the I.W.W.'s. They support the German-language periodicals. Their campaigns range from peace movements and anti-draft schemings to open efforts in favor of sedition and civil war.

These traitors are following out the vicious teachings of Prussian philosophers; there is no cause for surprise at their treasonable course. Unfortunately there is cause for surprise at the license which the Administration extends to their detestable activities. In this attitude the Administration is repeating its course of indifference to world-threatening aggression, and of submission to studied acts of murderous violence, which resulted, after two and a half years of injury and humiliation, in our being dragged unprepared into war.

If during those two and a half years a policy of courage, and of consistent and far-sighted Americanism, had been followed, either the brutal invasion of our national rights would have been checked without war or else if we had been forced into war we would have brought it instantly to a victorious end. Our failure to prepare is responsible for our failure now efficiently to act in the war. In exactly the same fashion it may be set down as certain that continuance of the present craven policy of ignoring sedition and paltering with treason will encourage and aid German autocracy, and will be translated either into terrible lists of Americans slain and crippled on the battlefield or else into an ignoble peace which will leave Germany free at some future time to resume its campaign against America and against liberty-loving mankind.

QUESTION

1. Who did Roosevelt believe threatened the United States at home during World War I?

21.4. HO CHI MINH (NGUYEN AI QUOC), PETITION TO WOODROW WILSON (1919)

During the 1919 peace conference in Paris following World War I, numerous individuals and groups from European and Japanese colonies petitioned the great powers to either grant independence or put them on a path toward self-determination, as promised by President Woodrow Wilson in his "Fourteen Points" speech of January 1918. Among these petitioners was Nguyen Ai Quoc, better known to Americans in the 1960s as North Vietnamese leader Ho Chi Minh. Ho Chi Minh presented this appeal to Secretary of State Robert Lansing in the vain hope that the United States would pressure France to liberate Vietnam, then called Annam.

To his Excellency, the Secretary of State of the Republic of the United States, Delegate to the Peace Conference
Excellency,

We take the liberty of submitting to you the accompanying memorandum setting forth the claims of the Annamite people on the occasion of the Allied victory.

We count on your great kindness to honor our appeal by your support whenever the opportunity arises.

We beg your Excellency graciously to accept the expression of our profound respect.

For the Group of Annamite Patriots
Nguyen Ai Quoc
56, rue Monsieur le Prince, Paris

CLAIMS OF THE ANNAMITE PEOPLE

Since the victory of the Allies, all the subject peoples are frantic with hope at the prospect of an era of right

Source: Department of State, 851G.00/1, National Archives, Washington, DC.

and justice which should begin for them by virtue of the formal and solemn engagements, made before the whole world by the various powers of the entente in the struggle of civilization against barbarism.

While waiting for the principle of national self-determination to pass from ideal to reality through the effective recognition of the sacred right of all peoples to decide their own destiny, the inhabitants of the ancient Empire of Annam, at the present time French Indochina, present to the noble Governments of the entente in general and in particular to the honorable French Government the following humble claims:

1. General amnesty for all the native people who have been condemned for political activity.
2. Reform of Indochinese justice by granting to the native population the same judicial guarantees as the Europeans have, and the total suppression of the special courts which are the instruments of terrorization and oppression against the most responsible elements of the Annamite people.
3. Freedom of press and speech.
4. Freedom of association and assembly.
5. Freedom to emigrate and to travel abroad.
6. Freedom of education, and creation in every province of technical and professional schools for the native population.
7. Replacement of the regime of arbitrary decrees by a regime of law.
8. A permanent delegation of native people elected to attend the French parliament in order to keep the latter informed of their needs.

The Annamite people, in presenting these claims, count on the worldwide justice of all the Powers, and rely in particular on the goodwill of the noble French people who hold our destiny in their hands and who, as France is a republic, have taken us under their protection. In requesting the protection of the French people, the people of Annam, far from feeling humiliated, on the contrary consider themselves honored, because they know that the French people stand for liberty and justice and will never renounce their sublime ideal of universal brotherhood. Consequently, in giving heed to the voice of the oppressed, the French people will be doing their duty to France and to humanity.

In the Name of the Group of Annamite Patriots
Nguyen Ai Quoc

QUESTIONS

1. What American ideals did Ho/Nguyen invoke in appealing for Vietnamese independence?
2. How radical or moderate were Ho's demands?

21.5. W. E. B. DUBOIS, "RETURNING SOLDIERS" (1919)

Like many African American leaders, W. E. B. DuBois (1868–1963), a founding member of the National Association for the Advancement of Colored People and the editor of *The Crisis*, supported American involvement in the First World War. DuBois hoped that shared sacrifice and military service in the struggle to make the world safe for democracy would lead to greater respect for the rights of African Americans at home in the United States. The wartime and postwar experiences of African American soldiers disappointed DuBois. This editorial from *The Crisis* urged returning African American soldiers to continue their fight for democracy.

Source: W. E. B. DuBois, "Returning Soldiers," *The Crisis* 18 (May 1919): 13–14.

We are returning from war! *The Crisis* and tens of thousands of black men were drafted into a great struggle. For bleeding France and what she means and has meant and will mean to us and humanity and against the threat of German race arrogance, we fought gladly and to the last drop of blood; for America and her highest ideals, we fought in far-off hope; for the dominant southern oligarchy entrenched in Washington, we fought in bitter resignation. For the America that represents and gloats in lynching, disfranchisement, caste, brutality and devilish insult—for this, in the hateful upturning and mixing of things, we were forced by vindictive fate to fight, also.

But today we return! We return from the slavery of uniform which the world's madness demanded us to don to the freedom of civil garb. We stand again to look America squarely in the face and call a spade a spade. We sing: This country of ours, despite all its better souls have done and dreamed, is yet a shameful land.

It *lynches.*

And lynching is barbarism of a degree of contemptible nastiness unparalleled in human history. Yet for fifty years we have lynched two Negroes a week, and we have kept this up right through the war.

It *disfranchises* its own citizens.

Disfranchisement is the deliberate theft and robbery of the only protection of poor against rich and black against white. The land that disfranchises its citizens and calls itself a democracy lies and knows it lies.

It encourages *ignorance.*

It has never really tried to educate the Negro. A dominant minority does not want Negroes educated. It wants servants, dogs, whores and monkeys. And when this land allows a reactionary group by its stolen political power to force as many black folk into these categories as it possibly can, it cries in contemptible hypocrisy: "They threaten us with degeneracy; they cannot be educated."

It *steals* from us.

It organizes industry to cheat us. It cheats us out of our land; it cheats us out of our labor. It confiscates our savings. It reduces our wages. It raises our rent. It steals our profit. It taxes us without representation. It keeps us consistently and universally poor, and then feeds us on charity and derides our poverty.

It *insults* us.

It has organized a nation-wide and latterly a world-wide propaganda of deliberate and continuous insult and defamation of black blood wherever found. It decrees that it shall not be possible in travel nor residence, work nor play, education nor instruction for a black man to exist without tacit or open acknowledgment of his inferiority to the dirtiest white dog. And it looks upon any attempt to question or even discuss this dogma as arrogance, unwarranted assumption and treason.

This is the country to which we Soldiers of Democracy return. This is the fatherland for which we fought! But it is *our* fatherland. It was right for us to fight. The faults of *our* country are *our* faults. Under similar circumstances, we would fight again. But by the God of Heaven, we are cowards and jackasses if now that that war is over, we do not marshal every ounce of our brain and brawn to fight a sterner, longer, more unbending battle against the forces of hell in our own land.

We *return.*

We *return from fighting.*

We *return fighting.*

Make way for Democracy! We saved it in France, and by the Great Jehovah, we will save it in the United States of America, or know the reason why.

QUESTIONS

1. According to DuBois, how were African American soldiers treated when they returned from military service?
2. How should African Americans respond to this treatment?
3. What were African Americans fighting for in the Great War? How should they continue the fight?

21.6. U.S. ARMY, INTELLIGENCE TEST, ALPHA (1921)

After the United States entered the Great War in April 1917, millions of men quickly joined or were drafted into military service. Psychologist Robert M. Yerkes convinced the army he could assess the intelligence of raw recruits and select those suitable for officer training by administering a standardized "IQ" test. The tests clearly favored those men from wealthier, educated backgrounds and were later used as evidence to claim that most eastern European immigrants and African Americans were "subnormal."

TEST 8

Notice the sample sentence:

People **hear** *with* **the eyes** *ears* **nose mouth**

The correct word is **ears**, because it makes the truest sentence.

In each of the sentences below you have four choices for the last word. Only one of them is correct. In each sentence draw a line under the one of these four words which makes the truest sentence. If you can not be sure, guess. The two samples are already marked as they should be.

SAMPLES *People* **hear** *with the* **eyes** *ears* **nose mouth**

France is in **Europe** *Asia Africa Australia*

1. **America** was discovered by **Drake Hudson Columbus Balboa**
2. **Pinochle** is played with **rackets cards pins dice**
3. The most prominent industry of **Detroit** is **automobiles brewing flour packing**
4. The **Wyandotte** is a kind of **horse fowl cattle granite**
5. The **U.S. School for Army Officers** is at **Annapolis West Point New Haven Ithaca**
6. **Food products** are made by **Smith & Wesson Swift & Co. W. L. Douglas B. T. Babbitt**
7. **Bud Fisher** is famous as an **actor author baseball player comic artist**
8. The **Guernsey** is a kind of **horse goat sheep cow**
9. **Marguerite Clark** is known as a **suffragist singer movie actress writer**
10. **"Hasn't scratched yet"** is used in advertising a **duster flour brush cleanser**
11. **Salsify** is a kind of **snake fish lizard vegetable**
12. **Coral** is obtained from **mines elephants oysters reefs**
13. **Rosa Bonheur** is famous as a **poet painter composer sculptor**
14. The **tuna** is a kind of **fish bird reptile insect**
15. **Emeralds** are usually **red blue green yellow**
16. **Maize** is a kind of **corn hay oats rice**
17. **Nabisco** is a **patent medicine disinfectant food product tooth paste**
18. **Velvet Joe** appears in advertisements of **tooth powder dry goods tobacco soap**
19. **Cypress** is a kind of **machine food tree fabric**
20. **Bombay** is a city in **China Egypt India Japan**
21. The **dictaphone** is a kind of **typewriter multigraph phonograph adding machine**
22. The **pancreas** is in the **abdomen head shoulder neck**
23. **Cheviot** is the name of a **fabric drink dance food**
24. **Larceny** is a term used in **medicine theology law pedagogy**

Source: Carl C. Brigham, *A Study of American Intelligence* (London: Oxford University Press, 1923), 29.

25. The **Battle of Gettysburg** was fought in **1863 1813 1778 1812**
26. The **bassoon** is used in **music stenography bookbinding lithography**
27. **Turpentine** comes from **petroleum ore hides trees**
28. The number of a **Zulu's legs** is **two four six eight**
29. The **scimitar** is a kind of **musket cannon pistol sword**
30. The **Knight engine** is used in the **Packard Lozier Stearns Pierce Arrow**
31. The author of "**The Raven**" is **Stevenson Kipling Hawthorne Poe**
32. **Spare** is a term used in **bowling football tennis hockey**
33. A **six-sided figure** is called a **scholium parallelogram hexagon trapezium**
34. **Isaac Pitman** was most famous in **physics shorthand railroading electricity**
35. The **ampere** is used in measuring **wind power electricity water power rainfall**
36. The **Overland car** is made in **Buffalo Detroit Flint Toledo**
37. **Mauve** is the name of a **drink color fabric food**
38. The **stanchion** is used in **fishing hunting farming motoring**
39. **Mica** is a **vegetable mineral gas liquid**
40. **Scrooge** appears in **Vanity Fair The Christmas Carol Romola Henry IV**

QUESTIONS

1. How do such intelligence tests show a cultural or class bias?
2. How could the results of these tests be misused?

CHAPTER 22

A NEW ERA, 1920 TO 1930

22.1. VISUAL DOCUMENT: AUTOMOBILE ADVERTISEMENT (1920)

Car ownership and the culture associated with the automobile exploded in the 1920s, fostered by advertising in newspapers, magazines, and the radio. This advertisement for the Columbia Six, an American-manufactured luxury car, was published in 1920 and reflects new techniques used by advertisers in the 1920s to market products.

Source: Columbia Motors Company/Wikipedia

QUESTIONS

1. How does this advertisement appeal to a potential buyer?
2. What does the purchase of the Columbia Six promise to the buyer?
3. In what ways does this advertisement reflect the growing significance of the automobile in American—and world—culture?

22.2. ELLISON DURANT SMITH, EXCERPTS FROM "'SHUT THE DOOR': A SENATOR SPEAKS FOR IMMIGRATION RESTRICTION" (APRIL 9, 1924)

During the 1924 congressional debate over immigration restriction, South Carolina Senator Ellison DuRant Smith expressed opposition to any new immigration to the United States. He drew on popular pseudoscientific racial stereotypes to conclude that recent immigrants threatened American prosperity and democracy.

I think that we have sufficient stock in America now for us to shut the door, Americanize what we have, and save the resources of America for the natural increase of our population. We all know that one of the most prolific causes of war is the desire for increased land ownership for the overflow of a congested population. We are increasing at such a rate that in the natural course of things in a comparatively few years the landed resources, the natural resources of the country, shall be taken up by the natural increase of our population. It seems to me the part of wisdom now that we have throughout the length and breadth of continental America a population which is beginning to encroach upon the reserve and virgin resources of the country to keep it in trust for the multiplying population of the country. . . .

I think we now have sufficient population in our country for us to shut the door and to breed up a pure, unadulterated American citizenship. I recognize that there is a dangerous lack of distinction between people of a certain nationality and the breed of the dog. Who is an American? Is he an immigrant from Italy? Is he an immigrant from Germany? If you were to go abroad and some one were to meet you and say, "I met a typical American," what would flash into your mind as a typical American, the typical representative of that new Nation? Would it be the son of an Italian immigrant, the son of a German immigrant, the son of any of the breeds from the Orient, the son of the denizens of Africa? We must not get our ethnological distinctions mixed up with out anthropological distinctions. It is the breed of the dog in which I am interested. I would like for the Members of the Senate to read that book just recently published by Madison Grant, *The Passing of a Great Race.* Thank God we have in America perhaps the largest percentage of any country in the world of the pure, unadulterated Anglo-Saxon stock; certainly the greatest of any nation in the Nordic breed. It is for the preservation of that splendid stock that has characterized us that I would make this not an asylum for the oppressed of all countries, but a country to assimilate and perfect that splendid type of manhood that has made America the foremost Nation in her progress and in her power, and

Source: Ellison DuRant Smith, speaking to the U.S. Senate, April 9, 1924, 68th Cong., 1st Sess., *Congressional Record* 65, 5961–62. See also http://historymatters.gmu.edu/d/5080.

yet the youngest of all the nations. I myself believe that the preservation of her institutions depends upon us now taking counsel with our condition and our experience during the last World War. . . .

The great desideratum of modern times has been education—not alone book knowledge, but that education which enables men to think right, to think logically, to think truthfully, men equipped with power to appreciate the rapidly developing conditions that are all about us, that have converted the world in the last 50 years into a brand new world and made us masters of forces that are revolutionizing production. We want men not like dumb, driven cattle from those nations where the progressive thought of the times has scarcely made a beginning and where they see men as mere machines; we want men who have an appreciation of the responsibility brought about by the manifestation of the power of that individual. We have not that in this country to-day. We have men here to-day who are selfishly utilizing the enormous forces discovered by genius, and if we are not careful as statesmen, if we are not careful in our legislation, these very masters of the tremendous forces that have been made available to us will bring us under their domination and control by virtue of the power they have in multiplying their wealth. . . .

We do not want to tangle the skein of America's progress by those who imperfectly understand the genius of our Government and the opportunities that lie about us. Let us keep what we have, protect what we have, make what we have the realization of the dream of those who wrote the Constitution.

I am more concerned about that than I am about whether a new railroad shall be built or whether there shall be diversified farming next year or whether a certain coal mine shall be mined. I would rather see American citizenship refined to the last degree in all that makes America what we hope it will be than to develop the resources of America at the expense of the citizenship of our country. The time has come when we should shut the door and keep what we have for what we hope our own people to be.

QUESTIONS

1. What are Senator Smith's main justifications for immigrant restriction?
2. Who is an "American," according to Senator Smith?
3. How would an antirestrictionist counter Smith's arguments?

22.3. KU KLUX KLAN, EXCERPTS FROM THE *KLAN MANUAL* (1925)

The Ku Klux Klan of the 1920s was explicitly antiblack, anti-Catholic, and anti-Jewish. These selections from the 1925 *Klan Manual* illuminate several of the Klan's objectives and methods.

OBJECTS AND PURPOSES (ARTICLE II, THE CONSTITUTION)

I. Mobilization

This is its primary purpose: "To unite white male persons, native-born, Gentile citizens of the United States of America, who owe no allegiance of any nature or degree to any foreign government, nation, institution, sect, ruler, person, or people; whose morals are good; whose reputations and vocations are respectable; whose habits are exemplary; who are of sound minds and eighteen years or more of age, under a common oath into a brotherhood of strict regulations."

Source: David Rothman and Sheila M. Rothman, eds., *Sources of the American Social Tradition* (New York: Basic Books, 1975), 2:166–172.

II. Cultural

The Knights of the Ku Klux Klan is a movement devoting itself to the needed task of developing a genuine spirit of American patriotism. Klansmen are to be examples of pure patriotism. They are to organize the patriotic sentiment of native-born white, Protestant Americans for the defense of distinctively American institutions. Klansmen are dedicated to the principle that America shall be made American through the promulgation of American doctrines, the dissemination of American ideals, the creation of wholesome American sentiment, the preservation of American institutions. . . .

IV. Beneficent

"To relieve the injured and the oppressed; to succor the suffering and unfortunate, especially widows and orphans."

The supreme pattern for all true Klansmen is their Criterion of Character, Jesus Christ, "who went about doing good." The movement accepts the full Christian program of unselfish helpfulness, and will seek to carry it on in the manner commanded by the one Master of Men, Christ Jesus.

V. Protective

1. The Home. "To Shield the Sanctity of the Home." The American home is fundamental to all that is best in life, in society, in church, and in the nation. It is the most sacred of human institutions. Its sanctity is to be preserved, its interests are to be safeguarded, and its well-being is to be promoted. Every influence that seeks to disrupt the home must itself be destroyed. The Knights of the Ku Klux Klan would protect the home by promoting whatever would make for its stability, its betterment, its safety, and its inviolability.

2. Womanhood. The Knights of the Ku Klux Klan declares that it is committed to "the sacred duty of protecting womanhood"; and announces that one of its purposes is "to shield . . . the chastity of womanhood."

The degradation of women is a violation of the sacredness of human personality, a sin against the race, a crime against society, a menace to our country, and a prostitution of all that is best, and noblest, and highest in life. No race, or society, or country, can rise higher than its womanhood.

3. The Helpless. "To protect the weak, the innocent, and the defenseless from the indignities, wrongs, and outrages of the lawless, the violent, and the brutal."

Children, the disabled, and other helpless ones are to know the protective, sheltering arms of the Klan.

VI. Racial

"To maintain forever white supremacy." "To maintain forever the God-given supremacy of the white race."

Every Klansman has unqualifiedly affirmed that he will "faithfully strive for the eternal maintenance of white supremacy."

THE OATH OF ALLEGIANCE

This oath of allegiance is divided into four sections, and will be analyzed section by section.

I. Obedience

Every Klansman, by his own oath, is solemnly and unconditionally pledged:

1. To obey faithfully the Constitution and laws of the order.
2. To conform to all regulations, usages, and requirements of the order.
3. To respect and support the Imperial Authority of the order.
4. To heed heartily.
5. The only qualification: "I having knowledge of same, Providence alone preventing." This is the only qualification that mitigates in any way the failure of any Klansman to keep any part of this section of the oath of allegiance.

II. Secrecy

1. *The Klansman's pledge of secrecy pertains to all matters connected with the Knights of the Ku Klux Klan.*
   (a) He is sworn to keep solemnly secret the symbols of the order. This means that he will not disclose the signs, words, or grip.
   (b) He is solemnly sworn to keep sacredly secret all information that he may receive concerning the order. The alien world is eager to learn all it can of the inner secrets and workings and plans of the organization. The Klansman who is enlightened as to these matters is obligated to keep his information both sacred and secret.

2. These matters must never be divulged to the alien. Klansmen must not publish or cause to be published such secret matters to any person in the whole world, except such person be a member of the order in good and regular standing, and not even then unless it be for the best interests of the order. . . .

III. Fidelity

1. *Every Klansman is solemnly pledged to guard and foster every interest of the order.*
   (a) He will protect the order in every respect. He will defend its honor. He will defend its principles. Every Klansman should be a propagator of the Knights of the Ku Klux Klan, disseminating its principles and promoting its growth.
   (b) He will maintain its social cast and dignity. Every Klan should be a body consisting of the best, most honorable, and outstanding men in every community. It is every Klansman's duty to live up to the highest and noblest standards prevailing among men of this character.

2. Every Klansman must be faithful in fulfilling all obligations to the order. He has pledged himself to pay promptly all just and legal demands made upon him to defray the expenses of his Klan and of the order, when same are due and called for. He will pay his dues, and will meet such other just demands as may be laid upon him, withholding nothing that rightfully belongs to the order. . . .

IV. Klannishness

1. *Civic and Patriotic*:
   (a) Every true Klansman is loyally patriotic. This means he is devoted to:
      (1) The government of the United States of America.
      (2) His state.
      (3) His flag.
      (4) The Constitution of the United States.
      (5) Constitutional laws.
      (6) Law enforcement.
   (b) The true Klansman is pledged to absolute devotion to American principles. Before the sacred altar of the Klan, face to face with the Stars and Stripes, and beneath the holy light of the Fiery Cross, he pledged himself in these words; "I swear that I will most zealously and valiantly shield and preserve, by any and all justifiable means and methods, the sacred Constitutional rights and privileges of . . ."
      (1) Free public schools.
      (2) Free speech and free press.
      (3) Separation of church and state.

QUESTIONS

1. How did the Ku Klux Klan define "pure patriotism"?
2. Who is an "American," according to the Klan?
3. What did the Klan fear most in the 1920s? How did the Klan address these fears?

22.4. CHARLES MERZ, "WHEN THE MOVIES GO ABROAD," EXCERPT (JANUARY 1926)

Beginning in the 1920s, Hollywood films dominated movie houses around the world. In this article, the author explores both the positive and the negative consequences of the popularity of American films.

There is no country in the world into which the American movie has not pushed its enterprising way and brought its gossip and its folklore, its sugary morals and its happy endings.

Listen to the warning of an Englishman: Lord Lee of Fareham told an audience in London recently that the American movie is a positive menace to the world. . . . "From your point of view as well as ours," he said, with his face turned toward America, "to send us trash of this description is fraught with terrible consequences not only in this country but in every country in the world."

This statement has been followed by other alarmist statements issuing from other British peers. Do such critics of American pictures show themselves too nervous?. . . .

For there is no question of the amazing reach of American films, or the completeness of their domination of the foreign market. . . .

For as Mr. Will H. Hays was accustomed to point out occasionally . . . the commercial importance of the moving picture reaches far beyond the theater, as "the silent salesman of American goods. . . ."

Automobiles manufactured here are ordered abroad after screen shadows have been observed to ride in them; China wants sewing machines; rich Peruvians buy piano-players; orders come to Grand Rapids from Japanese who have admired mission armchairs in the films. . . . Lord Newton tells the House of Commons that Yorkshire manufacturers of boots and clothing have been obliged to alter their plants because the Near East now wishes to dress like Rudolph Valentino. "Americans," asserts Lord Newton, "realized almost simultaneously with the cinema this heaven-sent method of advertising themselves, their country, methods, wares, even language, and seized on it as a method of persuading the whole world that only America matters."

Not unnaturally, the conquest has left traces of resentment. . . .

What does the foreigner see when the moving picture shows him the United States? . . . The America he sees is neither the America of Bryan nor of Barnum nor of Henry Cabot Lodge. It is an America of happy endings, goody-goody heroes, comedy policemen stumbling into man-holes, posses disappearing in the dust, bathing girls, and human flies. . . .

The problem is not vice but manifest absurdity. . . .

We may fairly ask if life exists anywhere (certainly it does not exist in the United States) in such stereotypes as the moving-picture magnate uses in his films. Such conceptions as he invites the rest of the world to entertain about America may be exhilarating to the young, but they do not make for much straight thinking as between one nation and its neighbors. If, as I have suggested, the first clear result of the movies' conquest is a trade war, the second is this muddying of international thought. . . .

The American movie is taking us into a new type of trade war largely without our knowing it.

Source: Charles Merz, "When the Movies Go Abroad," *Harper's Magazine,* January 1926, 160–65.

The American movie is caricaturing us cruelly enough to lay the basis for a libel suit.

But the American movie is also carrying a vast amount of decent and indecent fun into every back street of Europe and of Asia, into every kitchen where a woman cooks a humdrum meal, and into every factory where men look at the sun through smoky windows. It will probably never be made that vehicle of straight thinking which it is capable of being made. But the chance is there. For here is one medium which knows no frontiers. Language varies, manners vary, money varies, even railway gauges vary. The one universal unit in the world to-day is that slender ribbon which can carry hocus-pocus, growing-pains and dreams.

QUESTIONS

1. According to the author, what were some of the contributions of the popularity of Hollywood films abroad? What problems did these movies create?

2. What images do present-day Hollywood movies portray to the world? Are they positive or negative influences?

CHAPTER 23

A NEW DEAL FOR AMERICANS, 1931 TO 1939

23.1. VISUAL DOCUMENT: "HANDBILL OF VETERANS MARCH TO WASHINGTON" (1932)

During the summer of 1932, unemployed World War I veterans and their families traveled to Washington and camped out for weeks to demand payment of a promised cash bonus. President Hoover ordered the district police and army to disperse the peaceful "bonus marchers." This handbill marked a follow-up march on the Capital, following the election of Franklin D. Roosevelt as president the month before. Note the appeal to both Negro and white veterans.

Source: Veteran's Rank And File Committee. Veterans march to Washington to arrive at opening of Congress, December 5th, to demand cash payment of bonus. New York. New York, 1932. Pdf. http://www.loc.gov/exhibits/treasures/images/at0058g_2s.jpg

NEGRO

RANK and FILE

WHITE

VETERANS
MARCH TO WASHINGTON

TO ARRIVE AT OPENING OF CONGRESS

DECEMBER 5th, 1932

TO DEMAND

CASH PAYMENT of BONUS

**MARCH TO BE LED BY
RANK AND FILE VETERANS**

Again the veterans are going to march to Washington, to demand immediate full cash payment of the Bonus! This time we will have fighting leadership that won't sell us out. Why are we going to march? Let's see.

**A WINTER OF HUNGER
FACES THE VETERANS**

Cold, brutal winter is now on us. Over a million and a half unemployed veterans are hungry; hundreds of thousands of us have no shelter. And there will be more of us in that fix by the time winter comes.

Those of us who still have some work have suffered wage cuts, and the stagger plan, and face more wage cuts.

**INTEREST CHARGES
WIPE OUT BONUS BY 1945**

In 1945 there will be no Bonus for the rank and file veteran. The balance is now being eaten up by the compound interest charged by the government to all who borrowed the fifty percent of the Adjusted Service Certificate. In 1945 there will be only about $30 to $60 for the great majority of the veterans entitled to the Bonus. WE MUST FIGHT FOR THE BONUS NOW!

**THE ENEMIES OF THE BONUS
ARE UNITED AGAINST US**

The Republican, Democratic and Socialist Parties are all united in the fight against the payment of the balance due the veterans on the Bonus. They get the full support of the boss press, and the liberal writers, too.

Waters, the Hoke Smiths, the Doak Carters and other former leaders of the B. E. F. are fighting the rank and file veterans who are putting up a fight for the immediate payment of the Bonus.

The newly elected commander Johnson has had recent correspondence with Hoover and will not fight for the Bonus. General Glassford and the Hoover government are again preparing to prevent the veterans from making direct demands on Congress.

These fakers are all lined up with the enemies of the Bonus to prevent the rank and file of the veterans from uniting their mass power to march to Washington and again demand the immediate payment of the Bonus and fight against cutting of the disability allowance.

**RANK AND FILE VETERANS,
MARCH TO WASHINGTON!**

All Veterans March to Washington!

Veterans' organizations, elect Bonus Marchers. All rank and file veterans, including employed and unemployed veterans, should elect delegated Bonus Marchers. Veterans from shops, mills, mines, factories and farms should be elected. Bonus marchers should be elected from the veteran membership in labor, fraternal and social organizations.

**ELECT CITY RANK AND
FILE COMMITTEES**

City rank and file committees representing the various groups and organizations of veterans should meet to carry out the program of Central Rank and File Committee elected by the Cleveland Conference of the Rank and File Veterans. (Sept. 23-26.)

**HEROES IN 1917;
THEY CALL US "CRIMINALS" NOW**

In 1917 the government appealed to the masses: "Shall we be more tender with our dollars than with the lives of our sons?" (Second Liberty Bond poster, 1917.)

And now, in 1932: "The bonus marchers are criminals . ." (Statement of President Hoover.)

Neither then nor now did the Wall Street government care about the welfare of the soldier, "the lives of our sons."

Billions went to the billionaires who in 1917 made huge profits from the war, and today the billions go to the same crowd. The Congress that refused to give the starving veterans the bonus gave through the Reconstruction Finance Corporation four and a half billion dollars for the bankers, the railroads and other big corporations.

We got the bullets and the gas in 1917. Many of us were maimed and crippled for life. In 1932 we get the bullets and gas of the police, as we did in Washington, and of the troops, which Hoover called out against us.

Because we were demanding the Bonus so that we and our families could have something to eat, the President of the United States orders the army to gas and bayonet us, to burn our meagre belongings and to drive our wives and children out into the dark of the night

QUESTIONS

1. What assistance from the federal government did the veterans demand?

2. Why had they become so desperate by 1932?

3. Who opposed helping the veterans?

23.2. E. J. SULLIVAN, "THE 1932ND PSALM" (1932)

Shortly before the November 1932 presidential election, as the Depression grew worse, a despondent citizen named E. J. Sullivan published a parody of the twenty-third psalm. His words reflected growing anxiety about the nation's economy and ridiculed the response of Herbert Hoover.

THE 1932ND PSALM

Hoover is my shepherd, I am in want.
He maketh me to lie down on park benches
He leadeth me by still factories
He restoreth my doubt in the Republican Party.
He guided me in the path of the unemployed for
    his party's sake.
Yea, though I walk through the alley of soup
    kitchens, I am hungry.
I do not fear evil, for thou art against me.
Thy Cabinet and thy Senate, they do discomfort me.
    Thou didst prepare a reduction in my wages.

In the presence of my creditors thou anointed my
    income with taxes,
So my expense overruneth my income.
Surely poverty and hard times will follow me
All the days of the Republican administration.
And I shall dwell in a rented house forever.
Amen.

QUESTIONS

1. What real economic hardships did the author of this parody identify?

2. Why did the "psalm" attack Herbert Hoover?

Source: Robert McElvaine, *The Depression and New Deal: A History in Documents* (New York: Oxford University Press, 2003), 28.

23.3. U.S. CONGRESS, EXCERPTS FROM THE NATIONAL LABOR RELATIONS ACT (1935)

In 1935, Congress passed the National Labor Relations Act, sponsored by Senator Robert Wagner of New York. This legislation codified the right of workers to organize unions and bargain collectively with employers. The law, which was passed through presidential support and strenuous organizational efforts by groups such as the Congress of Industrial Organizations, resulted in millions of workers in the automobile, steel, coal, rubber, and electrical industries joining unions.

An Act
To diminish the causes of labor disputes burdening or obstructing interstate and foreign commerce, to create a National Labor Relations Board, and for other purposes.

FINDINGS AND POLICY

Sec. 1. The denial by employers of the right of employees to organize and the refusal by employers to accept the procedure of collective bargaining lead to strikes and other forms of industrial strife or unrest, which have the intent or the necessary effect of burdening or obstructing commerce by (a) impairing the efficiency, safety, or operation of the instrumentalities of commerce; (b) occurring in the current of commerce; (c) materially affecting, restraining, or controlling the flow of raw materials or manufactured or processed goods from or into the channels of commerce; or the prices of such materials or goods in commerce; or (d) causing diminution of employment and wages in such volume as substantially to impair or disrupt the market for goods flowing from or into the channels of commerce.

The inequality of bargaining power between employees who do not possess full freedom of association or actual liberty of contract, and employers who are organized in the corporate or other forms of ownership association substantially burdens and affects the flow of commerce, and tends to aggravate recurrent business depressions, by depressing wage rates and the purchasing power of wage earners in industry and by preventing the stabilization of competitive wage rates and working conditions within and between industries.

Experience has proved that protection by law of the right of employees to organize and bargain collectively safeguards commerce from injury, impairment, or interruption, and promotes the flow of commerce by removing certain recognized sources of industrial strife and unrest, by encouraging practices fundamental to the friendly adjustment of industrial disputes arising out of differences as to wages, hours, or other working conditions, and by restoring equality of bargaining power between employers and employees. . . .

Sec. 7. Employees shall have the right to self-organization, to form, join, or assist labor organizations, to bargain collectively through representatives of their own choosing, and to engage in concerted activities, for the purpose of collective bargaining or other mutual aid or protection.

Sec. 8. It shall be an unfair labor practice for an employer—

(1) To interfere with, restrain, or coerce employees in the exercise of the rights guaranteed in Section 7.
(2) To dominate or interfere with the formation or administration of any labor organization or contribute financial or other support to it. . . .
(3) By discrimination in regard to hire or tenure of employment or any term or condition of employment to encourage or discourage membership in any labor organization: Provided, That nothing in

Source: National Labor Relations Act, 29 U.S.C. §§ 151–69, https://www.nlrb.gov/national-labor-relations-act.

this Act . . . or in any other statute of the United States, shall preclude an employer from making an agreement with a labor organization (not established, maintained, or assisted by any action defined in this Act as an unfair labor practice) to require as a condition of employment membership therein, if such labor organization is the representative of the employees as provided in Section 9(a), in the appropriate collective bargaining unit covered by such agreement when made.

(4) To discharge or otherwise discriminate against an employee because he has filed charges or given testimony under this Act.

(5) To refuse to bargain collectively with the representatives of his employees, subject to the provisions of Section 9(a).

REPRESENTATIVES AND ELECTIONS

Sec. 9. (a) Representatives designated or selected for the purposes of collective bargaining by the majority of the employees in a unit appropriate for such purposes, shall be the exclusive representatives of all the employees in such unit for the purposes of collective bargaining in respect to rates of pay, wages, hours of employment, or other conditions of employment: Provided, That any individual employee or a group of employees shall have the right at any time to present grievances to their employer. . . .

LIMITATIONS

Sec. 13. Nothing in this Act shall be construed so as to interfere with or impede or diminish in any way the right to strike.

QUESTIONS

1. What support for labor unions did this law provide?

2. How did this support mark a change in government policy toward organized labor?

23.4. VISUAL DOCUMENT: SOCIAL SECURITY BOARD, "JOIN THE MARCH . . . TO OLD AGE SECURITY" POSTER (1936)

During 1936, American workers were encouraged by posters such as this one to sign up for their first Social Security card. A hallmark New Deal reform, Social Security held out the promise of a dignified retirement for the elderly and assistance to disabled workers.

QUESTIONS

1. What benefits did Social Security provide to most working Americans?

2. Who was excluded from Social Security coverage?

Source: "Join the March (1936)." Social Security Administration, Special Collections. https://www.ssa.gov/history/pubaffairs.html

23.5. VISUAL DOCUMENTS: DOROTHEA LANGE, PHOTOGRAPHS OF MIGRATORY WORKERS IN CALIFORNIA (1936–39)

Between 1935 and 1942, the Farm Security Administration hired some of the nation's most talented photographers, including Dorothea Lange, Sheldon Dick, Ben Shahn, and Walker Evans, to chronicle the lives of ordinary workers, migrant laborers, and rural farmers facing hard times.

Mexican Migratory Field Worker's Home on the Edge of a Frozen Pea Field, Imperial Valley, California, 1937.

Source: Dorothea Lange/U.S. Farm Security Administration/Library of Congress, Prints and Photographs Division.

Toward Los Angeles, 1937.

Migratory Workers in California, 1936–1939.

Source: Dorothea Lange/U.S. Farm Security Administration/Library of Congress, Prints and Photographs Division.

Source: Dorothea Lange/U.S. Farm Security Administration/Library of Congress, Prints and Photographs Division.

QUESTIONS

1. Why did Farm Security Administration photographers memorialize the poorest of the poor?

2. Who was the audience for these photographs?

23.6. TWO LETTERS (1936)

As American citizens suffered through the lean years of the Great Depression, they often found themselves having to do without the most basic necessities. New Deal programs helped many to regain their footing, but families still struggled to get by. The relationship President Franklin D. Roosevelt and First Lady Eleanor Roosevelt cultivated through their media outreach and demonstration of compassion for the poor led some citizens to contact the president and the first lady directly as they searched for assistance through hard times.

Anderson County Schools
Clinton, Tennessee
January 26, 1936
Mrs. Franklin D. Roosevelt
Washington, D.C.

My dear Mrs. Roosevelt,

You may think I am a very insignificant person to be writing to a person of your standing and ability but by reading your article and hearing your talks I know you are real and have an interest in people even my dear little needy boys and girls of the mountain schools.

I am Rural Supervisor of schools in my county. I have forty schools to supervise. Due to insufficient clothing and food many are unable to attend schools.

I wish it were possible for you to see some of the conditions. It is not uncommon for a child to have but one dress or one shirt. They have to stay at home the day the mother laundries them.

I am just wishing that in some of your groups that it would be possible to interest them in our needs. The Save the Children Fund, with headquarters in New York, has helped me some. Many children of my

schools would be unable to attend school had it not been for this organization.

I hope you will not consider me rude for writing. I have my heart in the work. I realize a *hungry or a cold child cannot learn too much.*

Yours very truly,

C. B. S.
Star Route One

Albertville, Ala.
January 1, 1936

Dear Mrs. Roosevelt,

For some time I have wished to be aqainted with you. Or merly to receive a letter from you. I haved wish much to see you, but as I am a poor girl and have never been out of our state that will be impossible I guess.

Mrs. Roosevelt since I have been in high school I have been studying modern things and conveniences. I took your family for my study. I have found the study to be the most interesting subjects I could have found. In the study I, at all times know where you are, by reading all papers I find at school and elsewhere. I

Source: Anonymous letter, 1936, in *Dear Mrs. Roosevelt: The Letters*, New Deal Network, accessed July 25, 2012, http://newdeal. feri.org/eleanor/cbs0136.htm ; and anonymous letter, 1936, in *Dear Mrs. Roosevelt: Letters from Children of the Great Depression*, ed. Robert Cohen (Chapel Hill: University of North Carolina Press, 2002), 105.

find what you are doing. You may never had given this a thought, but to think over our daily lives there is a good story to it.

My life has been a story to me and most of the time a miserable one. When I was 7 years old my father left for a law school and never returned. This leaving my mother and 4 children. He left us a small farm, but it could not keep us up. . . . I am now 15 years old and in the 10th grade. I have always been smart but I never had a chance as all of us is so poor. I hope to complete my education, but I will have to quit school I guess if there is no clothes can be bought. (Don't think that we are on the relief.) Mother has been a faithful servent for us to keep us to gather. I don't see how she has made it.

Mrs. Roosevelt, don't think I am just begging, but that is all you can call it I guess. There is no harm in asking I guess eather. Do you have any old clothes you have throwed back. You don't realize how honored I would feel to be wearing your clothes. I don't have a coat at all to wear. The clothes may be too large but I can cut them down so I can wear them. Not only clothes but old shoes, hats, hose, and under wear would be appreciated so much. I have three brothers that would appreciate any old clothes of your boys or husband. I wish you could see the part of North Alabama now. The trees, groves, and every thing is covered with ice and snow. It is a very pretty scene. But Oh, how cold it is here. People can hardly stay comfortable.

I will close now as it is about mail time. I hope to hear from you soon, (and real soon)

Your friend,

M. I.

QUESTIONS

1. What special bond did these Americans feel for Eleanor Roosevelt?
2. What kind of assistance did they request?

CHAPTER 24

ARSENAL OF DEMOCRACY: THE WORLD AT WAR, 1931 TO 1945

24.1. FRANKLIN D. ROOSEVELT AND WINSTON CHURCHILL, THE ATLANTIC CHARTER (1941)

In August 1941, four months before Japan's attack at Pearl Harbor, President Franklin Roosevelt and British Prime Minister Winston Churchill issued the Atlantic Charter. Reflecting Roosevelt's vision of a reformed world order, the charter spoke of bringing democracy, self-determination, and disarmament to the world following the defeat of the Axis powers.

THE PRESIDENT OF THE UNITED STATES OF AMERICA and the Prime Minister, Mr. *Churchill*, representing HIS MAJESTY'S GOVERNMENT IN THE UNITED KINGDOM, being met together, deem it right to make known certain common principles in the national policies of their respective countries on which they base their hopes for a better future for the world.

1. Their countries seek no aggrandizement, territorial or other.
2. They desire to see no territorial changes that do not accord with the freely expressed wishes of the peoples concerned.
3. They respect the right of all peoples to choose the form of government under which they will live; and they wish to see sovereign rights and self-government restored to those who have been forcibly deprived of them.

4. They will endeavor, with due respect for their existing obligations, to further the enjoyment by all States, great or small, victor or vanquished, of access, on equal terms, to the trade and to the raw materials of the world which are needed for their economic prosperity.
5. They desire to bring about the fullest collaboration between all nations in the economic field with the object of securing, for all, improved labor standards, economic advancement and social security.
6. After the final destruction of the Nazi tyranny, they hope to see established a peace which will afford to all nations the means of dwelling in safety within their own boundaries, and which will afford assurance that all the men in all the lands may live out their lives in freedom from fear and want.

Source: Declaration by Franklin D. Roosevelt and Winston Churchill, August 14, 1941, box 1, folder 7, President's Secretary's File. Courtesy of the Franklin D. Roosevelt Presidential Library and Museum Website, http://docs.fdrlibrary.marist.edu/PSF/BOX1/a07p01.html (2009).

7. Such a peace should enable all men to traverse the high seas and oceans without hindrance.
8. They believe that all of the nations of the world, for realistic as well as spiritual reasons, must come to the abandonment of the use of force. Since no future peace can be maintained if land, sea or air armaments continue to be employed by nations which threaten, or may threaten, aggression outside of their frontiers, they believe, pending the establishment of a wider and permanent system of general security, that the disarmament of such nations is essential. They will likewise aid and encourage all other practicable measures which will lighten for peace-loving peoples the crushing burden of armaments.

FRANKLIN D. ROOSEVELT
WINSTON S. CHURCHILL
August 14, 1941

QUESTIONS

1. What pledge did Roosevelt offer to colonial peoples?
2. What proposals did the document make to ensure postwar peace?

24.2. VISUAL DOCUMENT: JAPANESE ATTACK ON SHANGHAI (1937)

This photograph of a Chinese child injured in the Japanese attack on Shanghai in 1937 was widely circulated in the United States before and after the United States and Japan went to war in 1941. It created great sympathy with China's plight and cast the Japanese as savage aggressors.

Source: H. Wang, Bloody Saturday/Wikipedia

QUESTION

1. How can a photograph of devastation influence public opinion in ways that "factual" arguments and written documents about war and peace do not?

24.3. ELEANOR ROOSEVELT, EXCERPT FROM "RACE, RELIGION, AND PREJUDICE" (MAY 11, 1942)

During World War II, no American worked harder than Eleanor Roosevelt to preserve and advance the New Deal reform agenda. Americans fought racist dictatorships in the war against Germany and Japan but lived in a largely segregated country that barred the entry of most Eastern Europeans and Jews and all Asians. In this 1942 article, Mrs. Roosevelt spoke forcefully of the need to recognize the humanity of all peoples and assure their equality under the law. Even she, however, counseled patience by African Americans in asserting their full rights.

One of the phases of this war that we have to face is the question of race discrimination.

We have had a definite policy toward the Chinese and Japanese who wished to enter our country for many years, and I doubt very much if after this war is over we can differentiate between the peoples of Europe, the Near East and the Far East.

Perhaps the simplest way of facing the problem in the future is to say that we are fighting for freedom, and one of the freedoms we must establish is freedom from discrimination among the peoples of the world, either because of race, or of color, or of religion.

The people of the world have suddenly begun to stir and they seem to feel that in the future we should look upon each other as fellow human beings, judged by our acts, by our abilities, by our development, and not by any less fundamental differences.

Here in our own country we have any number of attitudes which have become habits and which constitute our approach to the Jewish people, the Japanese and Chinese people, the Italian people, and above all, to the Negro people in our midst.

Perhaps because the Negroes are our largest minority, our attitude towards them will have to be faced first of all. I keep on repeating that the way to face this situation is by being completely realistic. We cannot force people to accept friends for whom they have no liking, but living in a democracy it is entirely reasonable to demand that every citizen of that democracy enjoy the fundamental rights of a citizen.

Over and over again, I have stressed the rights of every citizen:

Equality before the law.

Equality of education.

Equality to hold a job according to his ability.

Equality of participation through the ballot in the government.

These are inherent rights in a democracy, and I do not see how we can fight this war and deny these rights to any citizen in our own land.

Source: Eleanor Roosevelt, "Race, Religion, and Prejudice," *The New Republic*, May 11, 1942, 630.

The other relationships will gradually settle themselves once these major things are part of our accepted philosophy.

It seems trite to say to the Negro, you must have patience, when he has had patience so long; you must not expect miracles overnight, when he can look back to the years of slavery and say—how many nights! he has waited for justice. Nevertheless, it is what we must continue to say in the interests of our government as a whole and of the Negro people; but that does not mean that we must sit idle and do nothing. We must keep moving forward steadily, removing restrictions which have no sense, and fighting prejudice. If we are wise we will do this where it is easiest to do it first, and watch it spread gradually to places where the old prejudices are slow to disappear.

There is now a great group of educated Negroes who can become leaders among their people, who can teach them the value of things of the mind and who qualify as the best in any field of endeavor. With these men and women it is impossible to think of any barriers of inferiority, but differences there are and always will be, and that is why on both sides there must be tact and patience and an effort at real understanding. Above everything else, no action must be taken which can cause so much bitterness that the whole liberalizing effort may be set back over a period of many years.

QUESTIONS

1. What racial problems did Mrs. Roosevelt identify in American society?
2. Why did she believe it was vital to solve these problems?

24.4. VISUAL DOCUMENT: WOMEN WORKERS GROOM LINES OF TRANSPARENT NOSES FOR DEADLY A-20 ATTACK BOMBERS (1942)

As sixteen million men entered military service between 1941 and 1945, American women faced greatly expanded opportunities and obligations. They worked in military production and became single parents, homemakers, breadwinners, and role models for their children. Women comprised nearly half the workforce in aircraft factories.

QUESTION

1. How did poster art of wartime women mark a reversal of feminine stereotypes existing before the war? What new realities did they reflect?

Source: Tango Images / Alamy Stock Photo

24.5. A. PHILIP RANDOLPH, "WHY SHOULD WE MARCH?" (1943)

World War II created a huge demand for skilled industrial workers, but factory owners were reluctant to hire African American workers to fill skilled—and therefore high-paying—positions. In 1941, A. Philip Randolph (1889–1979), the president of the Brotherhood of Sleeping Car Porters, proposed a march on Washington to demand fair employment opportunities for African Americans. In June 1941, President Roosevelt issued Executive Order 8802, creating a Committee on Fair Employment Practices and requiring factories that received war contracts to employ African Americans. Randolph canceled the planned march, but in this article from *Survey Graphic*, he calls for a series of protest rallies in cities across the nation to keep up pressure for racial equality.

Though I have found no Negroes who want to see the United Nations lose this war, I have found many who, before the war ends, want to see the stuffing knocked out of white supremacy and of empire over subject peoples. American Negroes, involved as we are in the general issues of the conflict, are confronted not with a choice but with the challenge both to win democracy for ourselves at home and to help win the war for democracy the world over.

There is no escape from the horns of this dilemma. There ought not to be escape. For if the war for democracy is not won abroad, the fight for democracy cannot be won at home. If this war cannot be won for the white peoples, it will not be won for the darker races.

Conversely, if freedom and equality are not vouchsafed the peoples of color, the war for democracy will not be won. Unless this double-barreled thesis is accepted and applied, the darker races will never wholeheartedly fight for the victory of the United Nations. That is why those familiar with the thinking of the American Negro have sensed his lack of enthusiasm, whether among the educated or uneducated, rich or poor, professional or non-professional, religious or secular, rural or urban, north, south, east or west.

That is why questions are being raised by Negroes in church, labor union and fraternal society; in poolroom, barbershop, schoolroom, hospital, hairdressing parlor; on college campus, railroad, and bus. One can hear such questions asked as these: What have Negroes to fight for? What's the difference between Hitler and that "cracker" Talmadge of Georgia? Why has a man got to be Jim-Crowed to die for democracy? If you haven't got democracy yourself, how can you carry it to somebody else?

What are the reasons for this state of mind? The answer is: discrimination, segregation, Jim Crow. Witness the navy, the army, the air corps; and also government services at Washington. In many parts of the South, Negroes in Uncle Sam's uniform are being put upon, mobbed, sometimes even shot down by civilian and military police, and on occasion lynched. Vested political interests in race prejudice are so deeply entrenched that to them winning the war against Hitler is secondary to preventing Negroes from winning democracy for themselves. This is worth many divisions to Hitler and Hirohito. While labor, business, and farm are subjected to ceilings and floors and not allowed to carry on as usual, these interests trade in the dangerous business of race hate as usual.

When the defense program began and billions of the taxpayers' money were appropriated for guns, ships, tanks and bombs, Negroes presented themselves

Source: A. Philip Randolph, *Survey Graphic* 31 (November 1942): 488–89.

for work only to be given the cold shoulder. North as well as South, and despite their qualifications, Negroes were denied skilled employment. Not until their wrath and indignation took the form of a proposed protest march on Washington, scheduled for July 1, 1941, did things begin to move in the form of defense jobs for Negroes. The march was postponed by the timely issuance (June 25, 1941) of the famous Executive Order No. 8802 by President Roosevelt. But this order and the President's Committee on Fair Employment Practice, established thereunder, have as yet only scratched the surface by way of eliminating discriminations on account of race or color in war industry. Both management and labor unions in too many places and in too many ways are still drawing the color line.

It is to meet this situation squarely with direct action that the March on Washington Movement launched its present program of protest mass meetings. Twenty thousand were in attendance at Madison Square Garden, June 16; sixteen thousand in the Coliseum in Chicago, June 26; nine thousand in the City Auditorium of St. Louis, August 14. Meetings of such magnitude were unprecedented among Negroes. The vast throngs were drawn from all walks and levels of Negro life—businessmen, teachers, laundry workers, Pullman porters, waiters, and red caps; preachers, crapshooters, and social workers; jitterbugs and Ph.D's. They came and sat in silence, thinking, applauding only when they considered the truth was told, when they felt strongly that something was going to be done about it.

The March on Washington Movement is essentially a movement of the people. It is all Negro and pro-Negro, but not for that reason anti-white or anti-Semitic, or anti-Catholic, or anti-foreign, or anti-labor. Its major weapon is the non-violent demonstration of Negro mass power. Negro leadership has united back of its drive for jobs and justice. "Whether Negroes should march on Washington, and if so, when?" will be the focus of a forthcoming national conference. For the plan of a protest march has not been abandoned. Its purpose would be to demonstrate that American Negroes are in deadly earnest, and all out for their full rights. No power on earth can cause them today to abandon their fight to wipe out every vestige of second class citizenship and the dual standards that plague them.

A community is democratic only when the humblest and weakest person can enjoy the highest civil, economic, and social rights that the biggest and most powerful possess. To trample on these rights of both Negroes and poor whites is such a commonplace in the South that it takes readily to anti-social, anti-labor, anti-Semitic and anti-Catholic propaganda. It was because of laxness in enforcing the Weimar constitution in republican Germany that Nazism made headway. Oppression of the Negroes in the United States, like suppression of the Jews in Germany, may open the way for a fascist dictatorship.

By fighting for their rights now, American Negroes are helping to make America a moral and spiritual arsenal of democracy. Their fight against the poll tax, against lynch law, segregation, and Jim Crow, their fight for economic, political, and social equality, thus becomes part of the global war for freedom.

PROGRAM OF THE MARCH ON WASHINGTON MOVEMENT

1. We demand, in the interest of national unity, the abrogation of every law which makes a distinction in treatment between citizens based on religion, creed, color, or national origin. This means an end to Jim Crow in education, in housing, in transportation and in every other social, economic, and political privilege; and especially, we demand, in the capital of the nation, an end to all segregation in public places and in public institutions.

2. We demand legislation to enforce the Fifth and Fourteenth Amendments guaranteeing that no person shall be deprived of life, liberty or property without due process of law, so that the full weight of the national government may be used for the protection of life and thereby may end the disgrace of lynching.

3. We demand the enforcement of the Fourteenth and Fifteenth Amendments and the enactment of the Pepper Poll Tax bill so that all barriers in the exercise of the suffrage are eliminated.

4. We demand the abolition of segregation and discrimination in the army, navy, marine corps, air corps, and all other branches of national defense.

5. We demand an end to discrimination in jobs and job training. Further, we demand that the FEPC be made a permanent administrative agency of the U.S. Government and that it be given power to enforce its decisions based on its findings.

6. We demand that federal funds be withheld from any agency which practices discrimination in the use of such funds.

7. We demand colored and minority group representation on all administrative agencies so that these groups may have recognition of their democratic right to participate in formulating policies.

8. We demand representation for the colored and minority racial groups on all missions, political and technical, which will be sent to the peace conference so that the interests of all people everywhere may be fully recognized and justly provided for in the post-war settlement.

QUESTIONS

1. What was at stake for African Americans in winning World War II?

2. What key demands did Randolph and march organizers make of the government?

24.6. FRANKLIN D. ROOSEVELT, EXCERPT FROM "AN ECONOMIC BILL OF RIGHTS" (JANUARY 11, 1944)

In his State of the Union address to Congress and the American people on January 11, 1944, President Franklin Roosevelt outlined the framework for a new economic bill of rights. Government, he proclaimed, must actively promote full employment, a decent standard of living, healthcare, affordable housing, and a good education. Many of these ideas were incorporated into the GI Bill of Rights that benefited sixteen million veterans and their families.

It is our duty now to begin to lay the plans and determine the strategy for the winning of a lasting peace and the establishment of an American standard of living higher than ever before known. We cannot be content, no matter how high that general standard of living may be, if some fraction of our people—whether it be one-third or one-fifth or one-tenth—is ill-fed, ill-clothed, ill-housed, and insecure.

This Republic had its beginning, and grew to its present strength, under the protection of certain inalienable political rights—among them the right of free speech, free press, free worship, trial by jury, freedom from unreasonable searches and seizures. They are our rights to life and liberty.

As our Nation has grown in size and stature, however—as our industrial economy expanded—these political rights proved inadequate to assure us equality in the pursuit of happiness.

We have come to a clear realization of the fact that true individual freedom cannot exist without economic security and independence. "Necessitous men are not free men." People who are hungry and out of a job are the stuff of which dictatorships are made.

In our day these economic truths have become accepted as self-evident. We have accepted, so to speak, a second Bill of Rights under which a new basis of security and prosperity can be established for all—regardless of station, race, or creed.

Source: Samuel I. Rosenman, ed., *The Public Papers and Addresses of Franklin D. Roosevelt* (New York: Harper & Bros., 1950), 13:40–42.

Among these are:

The right to a useful and remunerative job in the industries or shops or farms or mines of the Nation;

The right to earn enough to provide adequate food and clothing and recreation;

The right of every farmer to raise and sell his products at a return which will give him and his family a decent living;

The right of every businessman, large and small, to trade in an atmosphere of freedom from unfair competition and domination by monopolies at home or abroad;

The right of every family to a decent home;

The right to adequate medical care and the opportunity to achieve and enjoy good health;

The right to adequate protection from the economic fears of old age, sickness, accident, and unemployment;

The right to a good education.

All of these rights spell security. And after this war is won we must be prepared to move forward, in the implementation of these rights, to new goals of human happiness and well-being.

America's own rightful place in the world depends in large part upon how fully these and similar rights have been carried into practice for our citizens. For unless there is security here at home there cannot be lasting peace in the world.

QUESTIONS

1. How did Roosevelt propose expanding the concept of freedom contained in the Bill of Rights?
2. For what economic guarantees did he call?

CHAPTER 25

PROSPERITY AND LIBERTY UNDER THE SHADOW OF THE BOMB, 1945 TO 1952

25.1. EXHIBITING THE *ENOLA GAY*

Few events in history have generated as much controversy as the decision to use the atomic bomb on human targets. In the 1990s, the Smithsonian Institution acquired funding to restore the *Enola Gay*, the B-29 that dropped the bomb on Hiroshima. The American Air Force Association helped raise funds to support the restoration and presentation of the plane. After the airplane's restoration, the Smithsonian designed an exhibition, "The Crossroads: The End of World War II, the Atomic Bomb and the Origins of the Cold War," around it. Before the exhibit's official opening in 1995, Pacific veterans and politicians were given a sneak peak ahead of the public. Many came away dismayed at the impression left by an exhibit that included graphic details of the bomb's effect on the citizens of Hiroshima. Eight thousand veterans, with the support of conservatives in Congress, petitioned the Smithsonian to revise the exhibit and remove the disturbing content about bomb victims. The ensuing political fight was part of a larger "culture war" that pitted conservative politicians and pundits against historians. Ultimately, the exhibit was curtailed, eliminating most mentions of the politics of war and focusing on the mechanics of the airplane and its atomic payload. The director of the Smithsonian was fired, and a heated national debate about "who owns history" dominated the airwaves and front pages.

Source: Draft of *Enola Gay Exhibit*. Full text may be found in Philip Nobile, *Judgement at the Smithsonian* (New York: Marlow & Co., 1995); John T. Correll, "The Smithsonian and the Enola Gay," *Air Force Association Special Report*, Spring, 1994, http://secure. afa.org/media/enolagay/03-001.asp

TEXT OF FIRST DRAFT OF *ENOLA GAY* EXHIBIT

Ground zero:

Hiroshima, 8:15 A.M., August 6, 1945

Nagasaki, 11:02 A.M., August 9, 1945

Hiroshima, August 6, 1945

The mushroom cloud as seen 15 to 20 minutes after the explosion from the Mikumari Gorge, some 6.5 kilometers (4 miles) from ground zero. —Photograph by Seizo Yamada

"At first I saw rainbows, one over the other, then a mushroom cloud began to rise, and I heard the sound of a tremendous explosion." —Seizo Yamada, Hiroshima

(Artifacts in this section are preliminary; based on initial request to the Hiroshima and Nagasaki Museums.)

This wristwatch was smashed when its owner, Akito Kawagoe, was buried beneath the debris of the Futaba-No-Sato army barracks, 1.8 kilometers (1.1 miles) from the explosion. He escaped and survived. —Loaned by Akito Kawagoe and the Hiroshima Peace Memorial Museum

Broken wall clock, Nagasaki —Loaned by Nagasaki International Culture Hall

Hiroshima, 8:17. a.m., August 6, 1945

The base of the growing mushroom cloud as seen from near the Kanda Bridge, 8 kilometers (5 miles) from ground zero, two minutes after the explosion. —Photograph by Mitsuo Matsuhige

Hiroshima, 8:30 a.m., August 6, 1945

Gon'ichi Kimura was stationed at the Army Water Transport Headquarters, Ujina, about 4 kilometers (2.5 miles) south of ground zero. He snapped this photo of the cloud roughly 15 minutes after the explosion. —Photograph by Gon'ichi Kimura

Nagasaki, 11:12 a.m., August 9, 1945

This photograph of the Nagasaki cloud was taken from Koyagi Island in Nagasaki Harbor, 10 kilometers (6 miles) south of the explosion.

Nagasaki, 11:12 a.m., August 9, 1945

The Nagasaki cloud as seen from a spot only 8 kilometers (5 miles) from ground zero. Judging from the size and shape of the cloud, the photograph was taken about 10 minutes after the explosion. Twelve minutes after the blast, the top of the mushroom cloud had already reached an altitude of 12 kilometers (7.5 miles).

THE SMITHSONIAN AND THE *ENOLA GAY*

At the Smithsonian, History Grapples with Cultural Angst.

The Smithsonian Institution acquired the *Enola Gay*—the B-29 that dropped the first atomic bomb—forty-four years ago. After a decade of deterioration in open weather, the aircraft was put into storage in 1960. Now, following a lengthy period of restoration, it will finally be displayed to the public on the fiftieth anniversary of its famous mission. The exhibition will run from May 1995 to January 1996 at the Smithsonian's National Air and Space Museum in Washington.

The aircraft will be an element in a larger exhibition called "The Crossroads: The End of World War II, the Atomic Bomb, and the Origins of the Cold War." The context is the development of the atomic bomb and its use against the Japanese cities of Hiroshima and Nagasaki in August 1945.

The *Enola Gay*'s task was a grim one, hardly suitable for glamorization. Nevertheless, many visitors may be taken aback by what they see. That is particularly true for World War II veterans who had petitioned the museum to display the historic bomber in a more objective setting.

The restored aircraft will be there all right, the front fifty-six feet of it, anyway. The rest of the gallery space is allotted to a program about the atomic bomb. The presentation is designed for shock effect. The museum's exhibition plan notes that parents might find some parts unsuitable for viewing by their children, and the script warns that "parental discretion is advised."

For what the plan calls the "emotional center" of the exhibit, the curators are collecting burnt watches, broken wall clocks, and photos of victims—which will be enlarged to life size—as well as melted and broken religious objects. One display will be a schoolgirl's lunch box with remains of peas and rice reduced to carbon. To ensure that nobody misses the point, "where possible, photos of the persons who owned or wore these artifacts would be used to show that real people stood behind the artifacts." Survivors of Hiroshima and Nagasaki will recall the horror in their own words.

The Air and Space Museum says it takes no position on the "difficult moral and political questions" involved. For the past two years, however, museum officials have been under fire from veterans groups who charge that the exhibition plan is politically biased.

CONCESSIONS TO BALANCE

The exhibition plan the museum was following as recently as November picked up the story of the war in 1945 as the end approached. It depicted the Japanese in a desperate defense of their home islands, saying little about what had made such a defense necessary. U.S. conduct of the war was depicted as brutal, vindictive, and racially motivated.

The latest script, written in January, shows major concessions to balance. It acknowledges Japan's "naked aggression and extreme brutality" that began in the 1930s. It gives greater recognition to U.S. casualties. Despite some hedging, it says the atomic bomb "played a crucial role in ending the Pacific war quickly." Further revisions to the script are expected.

The ultimate effect of the exhibition will depend, of course, on how the words are blended with the artifacts and audiovisual elements. And despite the balancing material added, the curators still make some curious calls.

"For most Americans," the script says, "it was a war of vengeance. For most Japanese, it was a war to defend their unique culture against Western imperialism." Women, children, and mutilated religious objects are strongly emphasized in the "ground zero" scenes from Hiroshima and Nagasaki. The museum says this is "happenstance," not a deliberate ideological twist. The Air and Space Museum is also taking flak from the other side. A prominent historian serving on an advisory group for the exhibition, for example, objects to the "celebratory" treatment of the *Enola Gay* and complains that the crew showed "no remorse" for the mission.

QUESTIONS

1. Do you agree with the American Air Force Association that the exhibit plan was "politically biased?"
2. Is there a way to present such a controversial topic without cultural or political bias?

25.2. VISUAL DOCUMENT: *BRACEROS ENTERING THE U.S.* (1942)

In 1942, the United States and Mexico reached an agreement on a regulated worker immigration program to encourage Mexican workers to move north to jobs abandoned by the millions of American workers occupied by the war effort. The Emergency Farm Labor Supply, or Bracero Program, granted annual entry to hundreds of thousands of seasonal agricultural workers. This shift in attitudes and policy led to a fourfold increase in the Mexican-born population of California alone and permanently transformed the demographic character of the Southwest.

QUESTIONS

1. What was the Bracero Program? Why would a program like this have wide support between 1942 and 1964?
2. What historical information does this official government photograph of braceros entering the United States convey to the viewer?
3. Does this image convey a tone or a message you can discern? If so, what might the Department of Agriculture be trying to say to the American people with this type of public information?

Source: National Archives, Series: Historical File of the Office of Information, Department of Agriculture, 1900–1959

Record Group 16: Records of the Office of the Secretary of Agriculture, 1794 - ca. 2003. https://catalog.archives.gov/id/7452192

25.3. FRIEDA S. MILLER, "WHAT'S BECOME OF ROSIE THE RIVETER?" (MAY 5, 1946)

The systematic removal of women from the industrial workforce was more than a practical response to the return of male veterans—it was a Cold War imperative. Cold War government propaganda stressed that American women could best fight the communist ideological menace by being homemakers. Women's work in the Soviet Union and women's work in the United States became an important point of differentiation between the two systems. The Soviets celebrated women workers as symbols of socialist equality. American politicians pointed to Soviet women workers as an example of the backward communist system that required all citizens to slave away in service of the state.

WHAT'S BECOME OF ROSIE THE RIVETER?

Her Numbers Reduced by Millions since July, She Is Involved in a Tremendous Reshuffling

When a character captures the imagination of the American public, his ups and downs are followed with an interest that sometimes surpasses avidity. Thus it is with Rosie the Riveter, who symbolized to America the effort of all women workers toward winning the war.

Today, there is little doubt that Rosie and her industrial sisters are fading from the scene of heavy manufacturing. Since V-E Day, about a million women production workers have left the nation's aircraft plants, shipyards, ammunition factories and other industries that produced so prodigiously for war. The sharpest decline, of course, followed victory over Japan, but the trend had started even before V-E Day in the shipyards and aircraft plants, large wartime employers of women among the durable goods industries.

As a result of this exodus of women factory workers, the public is asking: Where have Rosie and the rest of the heroines of the war production front gone? What are they planning to do now that the men are taking over? Is it true that these women, despite their gallant war service, are finding factory doors to heavy industry closed to them?

Positive answers to all of the questions are not easy in a period of readjustment. Rosie and her sisters, like millions of men and women, have become involved in the most tremendous reshuffling of human resources, both occupationally and geographically, that the country ever has known. Some answers, however, have emerged with a certain clarity, and one of these is the whereabouts of Rosie the Riveter and the women for whom she became a wartime symbol.

Some of the former riveters and other industrial workers, wearied by the long grind of forty-eight hours and more per week and the exacting task of producing for war, are taking well-earned rests before putting out feelers about post-war jobs. Still others, particularly a number of the young women whose husbands have been demobilized from the armed services, have no definite plans. At the moment, they are waiting to see how their veteran husbands fare in the readjustments to civilian life.

If the ex-GI can bring home enough pay in his weekly envelope to support a wife and establish a home, the former Rosies will at least have the chance to devote their entire time to homemaking and some of them are sure to take it. On the other hand, if the husband wishes to continue his education, start in business for himself, or for some reason or another does not immediately resume his breadwinning role, the wife may find her pay check badly needed. In that event, she probably will seek another job, though the job in all likelihood will not be similar to her wartime

Source: Frieda S. Miller, "What's Become of Rosie the Riveter?" *New York Times*, May 5, 1946, SM11.

occupation, as disappointing as that fact will be—and has been to other displaced women war workers.

Some of the wartime factory workers, of course, already have new jobs—in consumer-goods plants, laundries, stores, restaurants, hotels, beauty shops and other civilian services. From records of employment, however, this number is not large, for the employment of women in all types of work has decreased by more than 4 million since last July, or dropped from about 19½ million to around 15½ million. In view of this large decline, the number of women looking for work— about half a million, according to the latest estimate— is surprisingly small, only 40,000 more than last July.

In the light of the long-time trend of women's increasing participation in the work life of the nation, this appears to be accounted for not by the fact that women as workers are showing a tendency to withdraw from paid employment but by certain characteristics of the present transitional period. Important among these are: (1) The reabsorption of returning service men; (2) the indecision of some workers, both men and women, concerning their future plans; (3) the lack of job opportunities commensurate with the skills and wages of displaced women; (4) the desire of some displaced workers to take a rest before looking for jobs; and (5) the expected voluntary withdrawal of large numbers of women who were duration workers. Other factors contributing to the decline in the number of women workers during the period from last July to the present were the withdrawal of seasonal workers and teenagers.

Much has been written and said about the fact that reconverted heavy industries are closing their doors, for the most part, to the very women they depended on during the war. This frequently has been referred to as marking "the end of industry's courtship of women workers." Undoubtedly, heavy industry no longer is courting the riveters, the welders and machine operators who helped to make victory possible, and in this fact may be reflected some of the prejudice that has been leveled at women by certain sections of industry. The inference, however, that prejudice alone accounts for the trek of women from the war plants is both unfair and unsound.

Prior to the war, women were less than 1 percent of the wage-earners in the ship-building industry. Women riveters, welders or crane operators would have been considered by some employers as fanciful as a tale from the "Arabian Nights." Yet, during the war, women production workers in commercial and Navy yards reached a peak of about 150,000. In the aircraft industry, which had only 4,000 women factory workers the week before the Pearl Harbor attack, the number rose to over 360,000, and women became more than a third of all workers producing such giants of the air as Liberators, B-29's, and the swift fighters that helped to spell victory.

Today, with peace at hand, our nation no longer needs these ships of war or the vast army of men and women who produced them. Women, relatively speaking, were newcomers to the shipyards and aircraft plants and, as such, were the first to feel the impact of cutbacks. Additionally, there were scores of factories that owed their very existence to war. Foremost among these were the ammunition plants, in which women formed more than 41 percent of all workers. Obviously, many of these factories have no peacetime future.

Women workers themselves, for the most part, are cognizant of the workings of the seniority system under which American industry operates. Since they generally were the last to come, it came as no surprise to them that they were the first to go. Most of them, however, liked the new and shining factories of which they became a part. They like the up-to-date equipment, the comfortable dressing rooms, the music that came to them through the loudspeaker system.

But more than the refinements, they liked the regular and higher pay that came in their weekly envelopes. It is in the pay that is being offered them with the current opening that they are most disappointed. This interest in the pay check is not peculiar to their sex. It is, as one woman riveter put it, "just the plain American desire to get ahead."

Women workers do not want to get ahead at the expense of veterans. In fact, they never have regarded their work as a substitute for that of men. Their won record of achievement over a long period of years obviates that need or desire. Even before the war, they were a fourth of all the nation's employed persons, and a half or more of those engaged in domestic service, medical and other health services, educational services, telephone services, hotels and lodging places, limited price variety stores, general merchandise stores, and in the manufacture of apparel and accessories, tobacco, knit goods and miscellaneous products made from textiles.

Contrary to the opinion held by many persons, even during the height of our spectacular war production, the bulk of the nation's employed women were hard at work on the kinds of jobs women always had performed. Unsung and unheralded, millions of women did their part for victory by staffing the stores, laundries, restaurants, consumer-goods plants and other establishments and industries that gave necessary underpinnings to war production. The needs of these women, as well as those of the displaced war workers, must be taken into account in the various plans that are made for women.

Rosie the Riveter and her industrial coworkers, as it was pointed out at a recent Women's Bureau conference on the post-war employment problems of women, upgraded themselves during the war. They would like to retain some, if not all, of the gains. Because expanding opportunities for women appear to be in the extension of established services and in the development of new services that post-war America will want and need rather than in the old-line industries in which men have predominated, the industrial workers' gains may not be measured in terms of retaining their war-acquired skills. If America accepts the challenge, they can be measured in other terms: Wages that permit them to maintain the standards of living they have achieved, hours of work that are conducive to health and decency standards, and working environments that are a far cry from those of some pre-war establishments.

Closely related to the question of wages is the matter of equal pay, or objective rates based on the content of the job rather than on the sex of the worker. As Senator Wayne Morse, co-author of the pending Federal equal-pay legislation, has pointed out, the principle of equal pay goes far beyond being a matter of plain justice to women. Because it rests on a sound economic basis, such a practice promotes the general welfare of the community and the nation by promoting wage levels and sustaining the purchasing power of all concerned. Women's awareness of this fact is one of the reasons why they feel that we cannot afford the threat that unequal pay to them involves. They have a deep, natural interest in the welfare of their families and realize that every time a working man's income is reduced through the competition of workers who can be hired at lower rates than those prevailing, the family of the man inevitably suffers a lower standard of living.

These needs of women workers have long existed, and for just as many years they have been recognized by individuals and agencies interested in the welfare of the wage-earning woman. Through concerted action notable gains have been made in minimum-wage legislation, in State equal-pay laws, and through other measures sponsored by unions and progressive employers. A great deal, however, remains to be done before Rosie the Riveter, Winnie the Welder, and other women of the war sorority of industrial workers will be content to return to the woman-employing fields that are characterized by substandard wages and unreasonably long hours.

These changes are needed not only for the sake of Rosie and other returning war workers but for the benefit of the thousands of women who stuck to their jobs in the service industries throughout the war. The plight of Rosie and her highly praised war companions may serve, however, to focus public attention on the issue. Club women, unions and other champions of women already have made considerable progress in this direction, and a few individual communities—though not nearly enough—are including women in their programs for post-war workers.

Secretary of Labor Schwellenbach, in an address before key representatives of more than 70 organizations who attended a recent Women's Bureau conference on the employment problems of women summed up the needs of women workers and issued a challenge to post-war America when he said:

"Certain artificial restrictions that belong to a past age should not be allowed to handicap the contribution women can make . . . for instance, no bars should be erected against the employment of women, married or single, in work they can do under physically healthful conditions***no pay scales should discriminate against them. As members of a free society, women should be enabled to choose the way of life that permits them to make their fullest contribution to the world's upbuilding."

QUESTIONS

1. What are some of the options indicated for the former "Rosies" in the postwar economy?
2. How does the article explain the striking decline in women workers?
3. Do the statistics on types of wartime employment change your perception of women workers during World War II?

25.4. W. E. B. DUBOIS, EXCERPTS FROM "AN APPEAL TO THE WORLD" (1947)

America's leading black intellectual, W. E. B. DuBois, eloquently captured African Americans' concerns about the coming Cold War. In an address entitled "An Appeal to the World: A Statement on the Denial of Human Rights to Minorities and an Appeal to the United Nations for Redress," presented to the United Nations General Assembly in 1947, DuBois presented research on the impact of segregation and the denial of voting rights on African Americans in the United States. DuBois's appeal presented American racism and Cold War hypocrisy in rich detail, with eloquence and insight not easily dismissed. Partly as a response to this plea for global recognition of American inequality, President Harry Truman created the first Civil Rights Commission. DuBois followed his United Nations address with an equally eloquent attack on American foreign policy at the World Peace Congress in April 1949.

W. E. B. Du Bois Papers (MS 312). Special Collections and University Archives, University of Massachusetts Amherst Libraries.

Source: Eric J. Sundquist, *The Oxford W. E. B. Du Bois Reader* (New York: Oxford University Press, 1996), 454–60.

There were in the United States of America, 1940, 12,865,518 citizens and residents, something less than a tenth of the nation, who form largely a segregated caste, with restricted legal rights, and many illegal disabilities. They are descendants of the Africans brought to America during the sixteenth, seventeenth, eighteenth and nineteenth centuries and reduced to slave labor. This group has no complete biological unity, but varies in color from white to black, and comprises a great variety of physical characteristics since many are the offspring of white European-Americans as well as of Africans and American Indians. There are a large number of white Americans who also descend from Negroes but who are not counted in the colored group nor subjected to caste restrictions because the preponderance of white blood conceals their descent.

The so-called American Negro group therefore, while it is in no sense absolutely set off physically from its fellow Americans, has nevertheless a strong, hereditary cultural unity, born of slavery, of common suffering, prolonged proscription and curtailment of political and civil rights; and especially because of economic and social disabilities. Largely from this fact, have arisen their cultural gifts to America—their rhythm, music and folk song; their religious faith and customs; their contribution to American art and literature; their defense of their country in every war, on land, sea and in the air; and especially the hard, continuous toil upon which the prosperity and wealth of this continent has largely been built.

The group has long been internally divided by dilemma as to whether its striving upward should be aimed at strengthening its inner cultural and group bonds, both for intrinsic progress and for offensive power against caste; or whether it should seek escape wherever and however possible into the surrounding American culture. Decision in this matter has been largely determined by outer compulsion rather than inner plan; for prolonged policies of segregation and discrimination have involuntarily welded the mass almost into a nation within a nation with its own schools, churches, hospitals, newspapers and many business enterprises.

The result has been to make American Negroes to a wide extent provincial, introvertive, self-conscious and narrowly race-loyal; but it has also inspired them to frantic and often successful effort to achieve, to deserve, to show the world their capacity to share modern civilization. As a result there is almost no area of American civilization in which the Negro has not made creditable showing in the face of all his handicaps.

If, however, the effect of the color caste system on the North American Negro has been both good and bad, its effect on white America has been disastrous. It has repeatedly led the greatest modern attempt at democratic government to deny its political ideals, to falsify its philanthropic assertions and to make its religion to a great extent hypocritical. A nation which boldly declared "That all men are created equal," proceeded to build its economy on chattel slavery; masters who declared race mixture impossible, sold their own children into slavery and left a mulatto progeny which neither law nor science can today disentangle; churches which excused slavery as calling the heathen to god, refused to recognize the freedom of converts or admit them to equal communion. Sectional strife over the profits of slave labor and conscientious revolt against making human beings real estate led to bloody civil war, and to a partial emancipation of slaves which nevertheless even to this day is not complete. Poverty, ignorance, disease and crime have been forced on these unfortunate victims of greed to an extent far beyond any social necessity; and a great nation, which today ought to be in the forefront of the march toward peace and democracy, finds itself continuously making common cause with race hate, prejudiced exploitation and oppression of the common man. Its high and noble words are turned against it, because they are contradicted in every syllable by the treatment of the American Negro for three hundred and twenty-eight years. . . .

Today the paradox again looms after the Second World War. We have recrudescence of race hate and caste restrictions in the United States and of these dangerous tendencies not simply for the United States itself but for all nations. When will nations learn that their enemies are quite as often within their own country as without? It is not Russia that threatens the United States so much as Mississippi; not Stalin and Molotov but Bilbo and Rankin; internal injustice done to one's brother is far more dangerous than the aggression of strangers from abroad. . . .

All these are but passing incidents, but they show clearly that a discrimination practiced in the United States against her own citizens and to a large extent a contravention of her own laws, cannot be persisted in, without infringing upon the rights of the peoples of the world and especially upon the ideals and the work of the United Nations.

QUESTIONS

1. Why do you think DuBois took his arguments about American civil rights to world forums?
2. What is the relationship between the rhetoric of the Cold War and the civil rights movement?
3. Was DuBois's strategy of strongly criticizing the United States in global forums wise?

CHAPTER 26

THE DYNAMIC 1950S, 1950 TO 1959

26.1. BILLY GRAHAM, EXCERPTS FROM A RE-ENVISIONING OF JONATHAN EDWARDS'S "SINNERS IN THE HANDS OF AN ANGRY GOD" FOR THE COLD WAR GENERATION (1949)

In late 1949, Christian evangelist Billy Graham initiated his first large-scale crusade in Los Angeles: an eight-week revival that, with the help of media giant William Randolph Hearst, launched Graham into America's religious spotlight. Graham often appropriated popular anticommunist rhetoric in his attempts to reinvigorate American society through vigorous preaching. Graham also drew on Jonathan Edwards's famous two-hundred-year-old sermon, "Sinners in the Hands of an Angry God," in his attempt to reform Los Angeles and convert anxious listeners.

No one, save Christ. Hear no voice, save God's. We pray that this mighty sermon that thou didst use 200 years ago might be used again in this day to stir thy people, to convict sinners. And we pray tonight that we might see such an outbreak in this place that we prayed for and dreamed of and called upon God for. We pray that thou would vindicate thy word tonight. And we pray that on this night might be the night on which all America is praying. In Jesus' name, Amen.

I've never stood before an audience in greater fear and trembling, and yet absolute dependence upon the Holy Spirit, as I now stand. And tonight, I covet, I request, the prayers of every child of God in this place.

It was 200 years ago, it was the year 1740. It was a cold, blustery day in New England, in Northampton, Massachusetts, when an aging man stepped to the platform before a congregation of people. The people were expectant, there had been a semblance of revival throughout New England, people had been praying, souls were being saved, thousands of Christians were being stirred, revival fires were spreading, very much as they are at the present time across America. Jonathan Edwards had his Ph.D. from Yale University. He was later to become the eminent President of Princeton University. Jonathan Edwards was one of the greatest scholars that America ever produced, one of

Source: "Billy Graham and Sinners in the Hands of an Angry God: A Digital Exhibit." © *The Works of Jonathan Edwards Online*, Jonathan Edwards Center, 2008–11, http://edwards.yale.edu/education/billy-graham.

the greatest preachers, a man of tremendous conviction, a man that we look back on today and revere, and pray that God might raise up again such men on the American scene, that will not compromise, but will preach the word of God seriously, like Jonathan Edwards preached. . . .

George Whitefield came over to stir the revival fires in that day. And what has been considered one of the greatest sermons ever preached by a man since the days of Pentecost, was one of the sermons that was used of God to shake New England in that day and age. The sermon was entitled "Sinners in the hands of an angry God." Jonathan Edwards stood before the crowd of people, hardly an eyelash moved, hardly a person moved a hand, and before he was through preaching, people gripped the front of the benches in front of them and screamed in mercy, and revival broke out that night.

Tonight, in the very strange providence of God, I'm doing something I've never done before in my ministry. I'm bringing to you that message that was preached 200 years ago by Jonathan Edwards, the president of Princeton University. I'm going to do as he did. He stepped to the platform, and with gestures he preached, but he read every word of it. It's a very brief sermon, it's not too long. I'm going to read it, and extemporize part of it, but I want you to feel the grip, I want you to feel the language. I'm asking tonight the same blessed Holy Ghost that moved in that day to move again tonight in 1949 and shake us out of our lethargy as Christians and convict sinners that we might come to repentance. So tonight, we take our text. I want you to see that scene, I want you to see the little lanterns. The little oil lanterns. I want you to see the candles in the windows. I want you to see the snow falling outside. I want you to see the people as they're sitting in this little auditorium. I want you to see this eminent man as he stands to his feet. And his opening words were these: "Let us turn to Deuteronomy

32:35." Deuteronomy 32:35. These words: "Their foot shall slide in due time." "Their foot shall slide in due time." And if you've ever listened in your life, I want you to listen tonight. I want you to listen to the text. I want you to listen to the message. "Their foot shall slide in due time."

I'll tell you tonight, the wrath of God is something. And God says, that judgment is coming upon this world. And God says, the wages of sin is death. And God says, the soul that sins shall die. Ladies and gentlemen, tonight, men and women, tonight every one of us are hanging over the pit of hell and the only thing that keeps us from dropping in is the mercy of Almighty God. And tonight, I'm glad to tell you something, because I'm glad to tell you this, that the Lord Jesus Christ died on the cross of Calvary, and that God loves you with an everlasting love, and the mercy of God is everlasting to everlasting. And I don't care who you are tonight, man, woman, boy, or girl, it makes no difference who you are tonight, the Lord Jesus Christ can cleanse you from sin, and you can be assured that you're going to heaven, and every man, woman, boy, and girl in this place to know they're saved before they leave this place.

Wouldn't it be wonderful to walk out with peace in your heart, and that you walk alone not be afraid of the next step, not be afraid that some place along the way tomorrow you're going to drop? Wouldn't it be wonderful to have that glorious peace and joy in your heart, knowing that your sins are cleansed, and you're ready to meet God? Well you can know it right now.

Right this minute. You say, how long does it take? Only an instant. You say, what do I have to do? All you have to do is let Jesus in, right now where you sit. You can make certain that you are ready to meet the Lord God. Shall we pray? Nobody leaving, nobody moving. You can leave while we were speaking, but not now. Not a person. Every head bowed. Every eye closed. While our heads are bowed, our eyes are closed, nobody's looking, I wonder how many people down in this place will say, "Billy, I'm not certain that I'm saved, I'm not certain if I died I'd go to heaven, I'm not sure how I stand before God, but I'd like to settle it, I'd like to know how I stand, I'd like to be certain that I'm on the road to heaven, I'd like to be sure that Christ lives in my heart. I don't want any doubts, I don't want any uncertainty, I want to know tonight that I'm on the road to heaven." All over this place—outside, nobody moving—all over this place, lift your hand tonight and say, "I want to be sure."

QUESTIONS

1. How does Graham close the chronological gap between 1741 and 1949?
2. What, for Graham, is at the heart of both Edwards's sermon and Graham's redaction of the same sermon?
3. How might have the perceived communist threat and the fear of atomic war impacted the audience who listened to Graham's call for conversion?

26.2. VISUAL DOCUMENTS: MARCH OF DIMES FUNDRAISING POSTER AND IMAGE OF IRON LUNGS IN GYM (1950S)

Efforts in applied science, especially in medicine, led to massive public health campaigns to eliminate infectious diseases during the 1950s. The dread disease of the age was polio. This insidious ailment struck children and teens seemingly at random and in their prime of life and health. Victims' symptoms ranged from partial disability to crippling effects so dire that patients were forced to be confined to a rudimentary artificial breathing device known as the *iron lung*. In 1954, Dr. Jonas Salk perfected the polio vaccine and became an international hero. Grass-roots citizen activism played a large role in the successful search for a cure for polio. The National Foundation for Infantile Paralysis was founded in 1938 to continue fundraising efforts begun by President Franklin Roosevelt. Volunteers began collecting dimes to support research, and the foundation was renamed the March of Dimes. Millions of people contributed dimes to support the research of Salk's team. This remarkable campaign featured affective posters of afflicted children and images of the dread iron lung. The March of Dimes set the model for fundraising for the rest of the century.

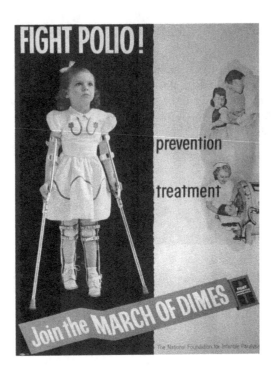

Source: March of Dimes Poster © March of Dimes Foundation

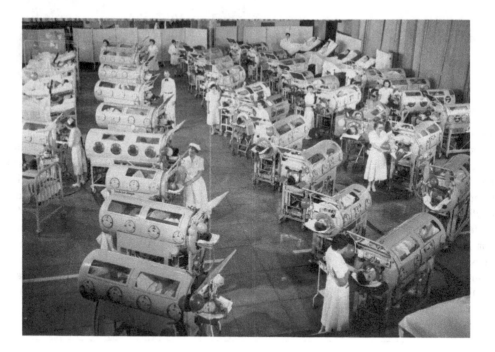

QUESTIONS

1. The picture of the large room full of iron lungs struck fear into the hearts of parents. Take a close look at the photograph. Does this appear to be a functioning treatment facility? If not, why would the photograph be staged this way?

2. Can you point to efforts in the early twenty-first century that clearly benefited from the cause-oriented marketing strategy pioneered by the March of Dimes?

Source: Bettman/Getty Images

26.3. DWIGHT D. EISENHOWER, ADDRESS TO CONGRESS ON THE INTERSTATE HIGHWAY SYSTEM (FEBRUARY 22, 1955)

The 1956 Interstate and Defense Highways Act, the largest public works program in American history, drastically altered cities, transformed millions of acres of rural lands, isolated some towns while elevating others, linked states, and facilitated the growth of suburbs and the complex of industries that sustained them. Missouri was one of three states (along with Kansas and Pennsylvania) to claim to be the first to begin construction on an interstate highway project following passage of the act.

FOR RELEASE AT 12 NOON (E.S.T.)

February 22, 1955

CAUTION: The following message of the President scheduled for delivery to the Congress today, February 22, 1955, MUST BE HELD IN STRICT CONFIDENCE and no portion, synopsis or intimation may be given out or published UNTIL RELEASE TIME.

The same caution applies to all newspapers, radio and television commentators and news broadcasters, both in the United States and abroad.

PLEASE USE EXTREME CARE TO AVOID PREMATURE PUBLICATION OR ANNOUNCEMENT.

James C. Hagerty
Press Secretary to the President

The White House

TO THE CONGRESS OF THE UNITED STATES:

Our unity as a nation is sustained by free communication of thought and by easy transportation of people and goods. The ceaseless flow of information throughout the Republic is matched by individual and commercial movement over a vast system of interconnected highways criss-crossing the Country and joining at our national borders with friendly neighbors to the north and south.

Together, the uniting forces of our communication and transportation systems are dynamic elements in the very name we bear—United States. Without them, we would be a mere alliance of many separate parts.

The Nation's highway system is a gigantic enterprise, one of our largest items of capital investment. Generations have gone into its building. Three million, three hundred and sixty-six thousand miles of road, travelled by 58 million motor vehicles, comprise it. The replacement cost of its drainage and bridge and tunnel works is incalculable. One in every seven Americans gains his livelihood and supports his family out of it. But, in large part, the network is inadequate for the nation's growing needs.

In recognition of this, the Governors in July of last year at my request began a study of both the problem and methods by which the Federal Government might assist the States in its solution. I appointed in September the President's Advisory Committee on a National Highway Program, headed by Lucius D. Clay, to work with the Governors and to propose a plan of action for submission to the Congress. At the same time, a committee representing departments and agencies of the national Government was organized to conduct studies coordinated with the other two groups.

All three were confronted with inescapable evidence that action, comprehensive and quick and forward-looking, is needed.

Source: Message to the Congress regarding highways, February 22, 1955, box 4, press releases February 8–March 14, 1955, Office of the Press Secretary to the President, Eisenhower Presidential Library

First: Each year, more than 36 thousand people are killed and more than a million injured on the highways. To the home where the tragic aftermath of an accident on an unsafe road is a gap in the family circle, the monetary worth of preventing that death cannot be reckoned. But reliable estimates place the measurable economic cost of the highway accident toll to the Nation at more than $4.3 billion a year.

Second: The physical condition of the present road net increases the cost of vehicle operation, according to many estimates, by as much as one cent per mile of vehicle travel. At the present rate of travel, this totals more than $5 billion a year. The cost is not borne by the individual vehicle operator alone. It pyramids into higher expense of doing the nation's business. Increased highway transportation costs, passed on through each step in the distribution of goods, are paid ultimately by the individual consumer.

Third: In case of an atomic attack on our key cities, the road net must permit quick evacuation of target areas, mobilization of defense forces and maintenance of every essential economic function. But the present system in critical areas would be the breeder of a deadly congestion within hours of an attack.

Fourth: Our Gross National Product, about $357 billion in 1954, is estimated to reach over $500 billion in 1965 when our population will exceed 180 million and, according to other estimates, will travel in 81 million vehicles 814 billion vehicle miles that year. Unless the present rate of highway improvement and development is increased, existing traffic jams only faintly foreshadow those of ten years hence.

To correct these deficiencies is an obligation of Government at every level. The highway system is a public enterprise. As the owner and operator, the various levels of Government have a responsibility for management that promotes the economy of the nation and properly serves the individual user. In the case of the Federal Government, moreover, expenditures on a highway program are a return to the highway user of the taxes which he pays in connection with his use of the highways.

Congress has recognized the national interest in the principal roads by authorizing two Federal-aid systems, selected cooperatively by the States, local units and the Bureau of Public Roads.

The Federal-aid primary system as of July 1, 1954, consisted of 234,407 miles, connecting all the principal cities, county seats, ports, manufacturing areas and other traffic generating centers.

In 1944 the Congress approved the Federal-aid secondary system, which on July 1, 1954, totaled 482,972 miles, referred to as farm-to-market roads—important feeders linking farms, factories, distribution outlets and smaller communities with the primary system.

Because some sections of the primary system, from the viewpoint of national interest are more important than others, the Congress in 1944 authorized the selection of a special network, not to exceed 40,000 miles in length, which would connect by routes, as direct as practicable, the principal metropolitan areas, cities and industrial centers, serve the national defense, and connect with routes of continental importance in the Dominion of Canada and the Republic of Mexico.

This National System of Interstate Highways, although it embraces only 1.2 percent of total road mileage, joins 42 State capital cities and 90 percent of all cities over 50,000 population. It carries more than a seventh of all traffic, a fifth of the rural traffic, serves 65 percent of the urban and 45 percent of the rural population. Approximately 37,600 miles have been designated to date. This system and its mileage are presently included within the Federal-aid primary system.

In addition to these systems, the Federal Government has the principal, and in many cases the sole, responsibility for roads that cross or provide access to Federally owned land—more than one-fifth the nation's area.

Of all these, the Interstate System must be given top priority in construction planning. But at the current rate of development, the Interstate network would not reach even a reasonable level of extent and efficiency in half a century. State highway departments cannot effectively meet the need. Adequate right-of-way to assure control of access; grade separation structures; relocation and realignment of present highways; all these, done on the necessary scale within an integrated system, exceed their collective capacity.

If we have a congested and unsafe and inadequate system, how then can we improve it so that ten years from now it will be fitted to the nation's requirements?

A realistic answer must be based on a study of all phases of highway financing, including a study of the costs of completing the several systems of highways, made by the Bureau of Public Roads in cooperation with the State highway departments and local units of government. This study, made at the direction of the 83rd Congress in the 1954 Federal-aid Highway Act, is the most comprehensive of its kind ever undertaken.

Its estimates of need show that a 10-year construction program to modernize all our roads and streets will require expenditure of $101 billion by all levels of Government.

The preliminary 10-year totals of needs by road systems are:

	(Billions)
Interstate (urban $11, rural $12 billion)	$23
Federal-aid Primary (urban $10, rural $20 billion)	30
Federal-aid Secondary (entirely rural)	15
Sub-total of Federal-aid Systems (urban $21, rural $47 billion)	68
Other roads and streets (urban $16, rural $17 billion)	33
Total of needs (urban $37, rural $64 billion)	$101

The Governor's Conference and the President's Advisory Committee are agreed that the Federal share of the needed construction program should be about 30 percent of the total, leaving to State and local units responsibility to finance the remainder.

The obvious responsibility to be accepted by the Federal Government, in addition to the existing Federal interest in our 3,366,000-mile network of highways, is the development of the Interstate System with its most essential urban arterial connections.

In its report, the Advisory Committee recommends:

1. That the Federal Government assume principal responsibility for the cost of a modern Interstate Network to be completed by 1964 to include the most essential urban arterial connections; at an annual average cost of $2.5 billion for the ten year period.
2. That Federal contributions to primary and secondary road systems, now at the rate authorized by the 1954 Act of approximately $525 million annually, be continued.

3. That Federal funds for that portion of the Federal-aid systems in urban areas not on the Interstate System, now approximately $75 million annually, be continued.
4. That Federal funds for Forest Highways be continued at the present $22.5 million per year rate.

Under these proposals, the total Federal expenditures through the ten year period would be:

	(Billions)
Interstate System	$25.000
Federal-aid Primary and Secondary	5.250
Federal-aid Urban	.750
Forest Highways	.225
	$31.225

The extension of necessary highways in the Territories and highway maintenance and improvement in National Parks, on Indian lands and on other public lands of the United States will continue to be treated in the budget for these particular subjects.

A sound Federal highway program, I believe, can and should stand on its own feet, with highway users providing the total dollars necessary for improvement and new construction. Financing of interstate and Federal-aid systems should be based on the planned use of increasing revenues from present gas and diesel oil taxes, augmented in limited instances with tolls.

I am inclined to the view that it is sounder to finance this program by special bond issues, to be paid off by the above-mentioned revenues which will be collected during the useful life of the roads and pledged to this purpose, rather than by an increase in general revenue obligations.

At this time, I am forwarding for use by the Congress in its deliberations the Report to the President made by the President's Advisory Committee on the National Highway Program. This study of the entire highway traffic problem and presentation of a detailed solution for its remedy is an analytical review of the major elements in a most complex situation. In addition, the Congress will have available the study made by the Bureau of Public Roads at the direction of the 83rd Congress.

These two documents together constitute a most exhaustive examination of the National highway system, its problems and their remedies. Inescapably, the vastness of the highway enterprise fosters varieties of proposals which must be resolved into a national highway pattern. The two reports, however, should generate recognition of the urgency that presses upon us; approval of a general program that will give us a modern safe highway system; realization of the rewards for prompt and comprehensive action. They provide a solid foundation for a sound program.

DWIGHT D. EISENHOWER
THE WHITE HOUSE,

February 22, 1955

QUESTIONS

1. Some historians have argued that interstate highways have done more to transform America than any other single phenomenon. Do you agree?
2. How does Eisenhower explain the connection between highways and national security?

26.4. KWAME NKRUMAH, EXCERPT FROM A SPEECH DELIVERED TO THE COUNCIL ON FOREIGN RELATIONS (1958)

In the aftermath of World War II, the map of the globe changed dramatically with the collapse of the European colonial system. Former colonies across the world sought and gained their independence from western European colonial powers. This trend was particularly evident in Africa and Asia and figured heavily in U.S. foreign policy in the 1950s.

Kwame Nkrumah, the leader of Ghana, the first of the former British colonies in Africa to gain its independence (1957), at first attempted to get support from the former colonial power and from the United States. In the early 1960s Nkrumah increasingly turned to the Eastern Bloc for assistance. Here is an excerpt from his speech at the Council on Foreign Relations, New York, in 1958.

[Principles:] The first is our desire to see Africa free and independent. The second is our determination to pursue foreign policies based upon non-alignment. The third is our urgent need for economic development. There is no area in Africa today where these three points are not on the agenda of politics. There is no need to underline for American readers the reason for Africa's rejection of colonial status. We believe, as do Americans, that to be self-governing is one of the inalienable rights

of man. In Africa, if peoples are to be truly independent, their governments must reflect the fact that, in all parts of Africa, the overwhelming majority of the population are native-born Africans. Even in the countries of considerable European settlement, such as Southern Rhodesia, 90 percent of the people are African. When, therefore, at our recent African conference, we called for an end to colonialism, we were doing no more than stating our belief that the fact of a vast African majority should be accepted as a basis of government in Africa (. . .)

We asked for the fixing of the definite dates for early independence and called upon the administering powers to take rapid steps to implement the provisions of the United Nations Charter and the political aspirations of the people, namely self-determination and independence. These steps should, in my view, include

Source: Jussi Hanhimäki and Odd Arne Westad, eds., *The Cold War: A History in Documents and Eyewitness Accounts* (Oxford: Oxford University Press, 2003), 354–56.

a greatly accelerated and enlarged programme of education and technical training, the opening up systematically of new opportunities for Africans in agriculture and industry and rapid growth of African participation in the country's political life. Such timetables would restore what, we believe, is most lacking in Africa's plural societies—and that is the element of confidence and hope on the part of the African majority (. . .)

Non-alignment can only be understood in the context of the present atomic arms race and the atmosphere of the Cold War. There is a wise African proverb: "When the bull elephants fight, the grass is trampled down." When we in Africa survey the industrial and military power concentrated behind the two great powers in the Cold War, we know that no military or strategic act of ours could make one jot of difference to this balance of power, while our involvement might draw us into areas of conflict which so far have not spread below the Sahara. Our attitude, I imagine, is very much that of an American looking at the disputes of Europe in the 19th century. We do not wish to be involved. In addition, we know that we cannot affect the outcome. Above all, we believe the peace of the world in general is served, not harmed by keeping one great continent free from the strife and rivalry of military blocs and cold wars.

QUESTIONS

1. Why does Nkrumah wish to maintain links to the United States?
2. How does the Cold War look different from the vantage point of a Third World leader?
3. White House photographers captured virtually all official events generating hundreds of thousands of images. If you "read" a basic official photograph like the one shown here as a source for history, what information might be revealed?

Source: Abbie Rowe. White House Photographs. John F. Kennedy Presidential Library and Museum, Boston

CHAPTER 27

THE OPTIMISM AND THE ANGUISH OF THE 1960S, 1960 TO 1969

27.1. HO CHI MINH, EXCERPTS FROM DECLARATION OF INDEPENDENCE (1945)

On January 18, 1945, in the final year of World War II, Vietnamese communist leader Ho Chi Minh sent this letter to President Harry S. Truman, "on the occasion of the first assembly of the United Nations in London." Minh had recently declared Vietnamese independence from France using the opening sentence of the U.S. Declaration of Independence as an appeal to the United States and its allies for support in the aftermath of the Japanese occupation. Minh had reason to believe this support might be forthcoming after working with the U.S. Military Office of Strategic Services against the Japanese in Vietnam. Despite these efforts, the United States declined to support Vietnamese independence and started supporting the French military effort to reclaim their colony in 1950 with the first of what became billions in financial aid. The letter praised the U.S. support of Vietnamese independence from France.

Hanoi January 18 1946.
President HO CHI MINH,
Vietnam Democratic Republic, HANOI
To President HARRY TRUMAN
UNITED STATES OF AMERICA
WASHINGTON D.C.
DEAR MR PRESIDENT,
On the occasion of the first assembly of the United Nations in London, I beg to congratulate you for the continuous and successful efforts your Government has been making to maintain Peace and Security all over the World.

As Peace is indivisible and as the Far East is being taken into especial consideration by your high Representative in China, General MARSHALL, I think it our duty to inform you on what is going on in our country and on what grave consequences for World Security the aggressive war inflicted upon us by the French may bring about.

Source: NATIONAL ARCHIVES 28469393 FILE UNIT: 800 INDOCHINA 1946, 1946–1948 SERIES: GENERAL RECORDS, 1946–1948 RECORD GROUP 84: RECORDS OF THE FOREIGN SERVICE POSTS OF THE DEPARTMENT OF STATE, 1788–1991. catalog.archives.gov/id/28469393

As early as 1941, Vietnam has risen up against the Japanese fascists, and taken arms by the side of the Allies. After the Japanese surrendered to the Allies, a Provisional Government was set up to restore order and eradicate all fascist intentions in Vietnam. Supported by the whole nation, it carried out a democratic program, and succeeded in restoring order and discipline everywhere. Under very difficult circumstances, general elections for National Congress were organized and took place on January 6th, 1946 throughout the land, including 9 000 000 electors of whom more than 90 percent went to the polls.

The French colonialists, on the contrary surrendered to the Japanese as early as September 1941. For four years they wholeheartedly cooperated with the Japanese to fight against the Allies and to repress the Vietnamese population. On March 9th, 1945, five months before the Japanese were defeated, the French by a second surrender, lost all right and control over Indochina.

On September 23rd, 1945, while the New Vietnam Democratic Republic was making strenuous efforts to carry out her reconstruction program, the French launched a night attack on the innocent population of Saigon, which was followed up by a systematically destructive murderous warfare. Facts of looting, assassination of civilians, violence, indiscriminate bombing of non-strategical places by war planes, are reported everyday. Their intention is to invade the whole country and to reestablish their domination.

In the meanwhile, after the offer of interference voiced by Mr VINCENT CARTER, Chairman of the Far-East Department, our people enthusiastically welcomed President TRUMAN's address on October 28 1945, in which he vigorously and concretely set forth the principles of self-determination and equality of status laid down in the Atlantic and San Francisco Charters.

Since that time, the French have tremendously increased their fighting forces. Millions of people will suffer, thousands will be killed and invaluable properties will be destroyed, unless the United States would step out to stop that bloodshed and unlawful aggression.

For this reason, on behalf of my people and Government, I respectfully request you to interfere for an immediate solution of the Vietnamese issue. The people of Vietnam earnestly hopes that the great American Republic would help us to conquer full independence and support us in our reconstruction work.

Thus, with the assistance of China and the United States, both in capital and technique, our Vietnam Republic will be able to bring her share in the building-up of World Peace and World Prosperity.

With respect
I am, dear Mr President,
Yours truly,
Ho Chi Minh

QUESTIONS

1. How does this very early document in the long history of U.S. involvement in Vietnam help us understand how the United States slowly became involved in this distant conflict?

2. How does Minh explain the efforts of the Vietnamese Provisional Government in the aftermath of the Japanese defeat in the region?

3. How does Minh conclude his message to Truman and why might he have used this argument?

27.2. VISUAL DOCUMENT: DAVID LEVINE, "VIETNAM: THE TURNING POINT" (MAY 12, 1966)

In the spring of 1966, President Lyndon B. Johnson opened his shirt to show reporters the scar from his recent gallbladder surgery. As opposition to the war mounted, David Levine drew a widely reproduced cartoon indicating that the president's real wound was thousands of miles away in Vietnam.

QUESTIONS

1. How does this cartoon visually capture a growing critique of the war in Vietnam?
2. Cartoons often outlast other forms of political communication. In what ways does a simple cartoon like this help us understand important historical debates?

Source: Walter Daran/Time & Life Pictures/Getty Images.

David Levine, "Vietnam: The Turning Point," *The New York Review of Books*, May 12, 1966. Walter Daran/Time & Life Pictures/Getty Images.

27.3. SENATOR SAM ERVIN, COMMENTS ON WATERGATE (1973)

North Carolina Democratic Senator Sam Ervin chaired the Senate Watergate committee. During the committee's televised hearings in the summer of 1973, Ervin explained why the issues in the Watergate scandal were so important.

I think . . . they were unable to accept the risk that people should exercise freedom for themselves. The First Amendment was written giving the rights of freedom of speech and freedom of thought, freedom of the press and freedom to protest to government, to make America a free society. . . .

I think one of the unfortunate things which have arisen in recent years is that too many men in power have too little commitment to freedom and actually fear the exercise of freedom by other people, especially people whose actions or thoughts are displeasing to them. . . .

I love my country. I venerate the office of the President, and I have the best wishes for the success of the incumbent of that office, because he is the only president this country has at this time.

But beyond that, the President of the United States, by reason of the fact that he holds the highest office in the gift of the American people, owes an obligation to furnish a high standard of leadership to this nation and his constitutional duties, in my opinion, and undoubtedly his duty of affording moral leadership to the country, place upon him some obligation in these circumstances.

And I don't think the people of the United States are interested so much in abstruse arguments about the separation of powers or executive privilege as they are in finding the answer to that question.

I deeply regret that this situation has arisen, because I think that the Watergate tragedy is the greatest tragedy this country has ever suffered. I used to think the Civil War was our country's greatest tragedy, but I do remember that there were some redeeming features in the Civil War in that there was some spirit of sacrifice and heroism displayed on both sides. I see no redeeming features in Watergate.

QUESTIONS

1. How does the author make the case for the broader significance of Watergate?
2. What is the most important consequence of Watergate, according to the author?

Source: Paul R. Clancy, *Just a Country Lawyer: A Biography of Sam Ervin* (Bloomington: Indiana University Press, 1974), 264–65, 279–80.

27.4. VISUAL DOCUMENT: HERBLOCK, *NIXON HANGING BETWEEN THE TAPES* IN *THE WASHINGTON POST* (MAY 24, 1974)

As the Watergate scandal intensified, President Richard M. Nixon responded to reports that he had paid only a few hundred dollars in income taxes with the remark, "I am not a crook." *Washington Post* cartoonist Herblock, a longtime Nixon critic, mocked his defense.

QUESTIONS

1. Can you point to the different historical issues addressed by this simple cartoon?

2. How does Herblock use visual clues to help address complicated debates about presidential power and authority?

Source: A 1974 Herblock Cartoon, © The Herb Block Foundation
Caroline and Erwin Swann Collection of Caricature & Cartoon, Library of Congress.

CHAPTER 28

THE VIETNAM ERA, 1961 TO 1975

28.1. STUDENTS FOR A DEMOCRATIC SOCIETY, *THE PORT HURON STATEMENT* (1962) AND AN APPEAL TO STUDENTS (1964)

In 1962, University of Michigan student Tom Hayden drafted the *Port Huron Statement*, the first official document of the newly formed Students for a Democratic Society (SDS). In it, SDS criticized hypocritical and unjust aspects of post–World War II U.S. society. On campuses across the country, SDS's presence grew in 1964 and 1965. Copies of the *Port Huron Statement* circulated widely, along with appeals to join SDS. The appeal to students appeared on the back cover of the second printing of the *Port Huron Statement* (December 1964).

THE PORT HURON STATEMENT

Introduction: Agenda for a Generation

We are people of this generation, bred in at least modest comfort, housed now in universities, looking uncomfortably to the world we inherit.

When we were kids the United States was the wealthiest and strongest country in the world; the only one with the atom bomb, the least scarred by modern war, an initiator of the United Nations that we thought would distribute Western influence throughout the world. Freedom and equality for each individual, government of, by, and for the people—these American values we found good, principles by which we could live as men. Many of us began maturing in complacency.

As we grew, however, our comfort was penetrated by events too troubling to dismiss. First, the permeating and victimizing fact of human degradation, symbolized by the Southern struggle against racial bigotry, compelled most of us from silence to activism. Second, the enclosing fact of the Cold War, symbolized by the presence of the Bomb, brought awareness that we ourselves, and our friends, and millions of abstract "others" we knew more directly because of our common peril, might die at any time. We might deliberately ignore, or avoid, or fail to feel all other human problems, but not these two, for these were too immediate and crushing in their impact, too challenging in the demand that we as individuals take the responsibility for encounter and resolution.

Source: Students for a Democratic Society, *The Port Huron Statement* (1962; repr. Chicago: Charles S. Kerr, 1999), 7–8.

While these and other problems either directly oppressed us or rankled our consciences and became our subjective concerns, we began to see complicated and disturbing paradoxes in our surrounding America. The declaration "all men are created equal . . ." rang hollow before the facts of Negro life in the South and the big cities of the North. The proclaimed peaceful intentions of the United States contradicted its economic and military investments in the Cold War status quo.

We witnessed, and continue to witness, other paradoxes. With nuclear energy whole cities can easily be powered, yet the dominant nation-states seem more likely to unleash destruction greater than that incurred in all wars of human history. Although our own technology is destroying old and creating new forms of social organization, men still tolerate meaningless work and idleness. While two-thirds of mankind suffers undernourishment, our own upper classes revel amidst superfluous abundance. Although world population is expected to double in forty years, the nations still tolerate anarchy as a major principle of international conduct and uncontrolled exploitation governs the sapping of the earth's physical resources. Although mankind desperately needs revolutionary leadership, America rests in national stalemate, its goals ambiguous and tradition-bound instead of informed and clear, its democratic system apathetic and manipulated rather than "of, by, and for the people."

APPEAL TO STUDENTS

Students for a Democratic Society!

SDS is a movement of young people who study and participate in daily struggles for social change. Committed to change in many spheres of society, SDS members, in chapters, projects, and as individuals:

- Organize the dispossessed in community movements for economic gains. During the summer of 1964, one hundred and fifty students provided the full-time staffs for 10 community projects in the urban North—40 of them continuing full-time in the fall. Movements of welfare mothers, the unemployed, tenants, and others have been organized around their particular grievances.

- Participate in activity for peace through protest, research, education, and community organization. SDS organized protests and proposed peaceful solutions during the Cuba and Vietnam crises; sponsors peace research among students; and is undertaking pilot efforts to organize defense workers for economic conversion.

- Work for civil rights through direct action, publication, and support of the Student Nonviolent Coordinating Committee. SDS projects in Chester, Pa., and Newark, N.J., serve as models for Negro movements in the North due to their mass support.

- Inject controversy into a stagnant educational system. SDS participated in the mass demonstrations and organized national support for free speech at Berkeley; pioneered in the introduction of peace courses into college curricula; and initiated the union organization of student employees at the U. of Michigan.

- Support political insurgents, such as Noel Day in Boston, in the fight for a government that would promote social justice. SDS produces studies of the political and electoral situation.
  Won't you join?

QUESTIONS

1. How does the first statement explain the reasons for growing concern among young Americans?

2. Both documents point to a change that prompted some university students to question what they thought about their country. What was this change?

3. What is the relationship between the various activities stated in the SDS document?

28.2. SARGENT SHRIVER, "JOB CORPS COSTS" (1965)

Many Great Society programs drew criticism for their high costs. Sargent Shriver, the director of the Office of Economic Opportunity, the government's coordinating body for the War on Poverty, defends the Job Corps, a program designed to employ and train for work poor and poorly educated young people.

LETTERS TO THE EDITOR

Job Corps Costs

A news report in your paper recently made an adverse comparison between the total costs to the Government of providing 12 months of basic vocational and citizenship training to our disadvantaged youths in residential training centers under the United States Job Corps and the costs only to the student of an academic year at Harvard University.

The dollar costs in these two cases are not comparable, and not much else in the comparison is relevant. The comparison, in fact, is superficial, invidious and inaccurate.

Harvard students are among the most brilliant, self-reliant, and highly trained youth our Nation can produce. Thousands of dollars have been invested in their education before they ever get to Harvard. Most of them come from good schools and good families, and have lived in communities where much training and preparation has been given to them. The very atmosphere they breathe is helpful to them. They are getting advanced training at the top of our academic system.

Job Corps enrollees come from situations exactly the opposite. They have gotten the worst and cheapest training. Very little has been invested in them by their impoverished parents or by society. They frequently come from broken homes and physical environments conducive to everything but good work habits and good citizenship. The fact is that not only are they not qualified for Harvard; they are unqualified for any kind of job with a real future in America today.

These differences would lead an objective critic to anticipate much higher costs for producing useful citizens out of Job Corps enrollees. Surprisingly, the Job Corps costs are significantly lower, per person, per year than the Harvard costs.

At Harvard, according to a study made by Seymour Harris, the noted Harvard economist, in an article entitled *The Economics of Harvard*, the tuition actually charged the student is only one third the educational cost to the University. The cost of tuition and room and board to the student at Harvard is $2890, according to the 1964 Official Register. Add to this cost to the student the factors outlined by Seymour Harris and you get $6410 per annum as the cost of an academic-year Harvard education.

On the other hand, the total cost to the Government for a Job Corps enrollee for nine months is only $4650—about two thirds of the cost of a Harvard education, and this figure includes $1500 for allowances, travel, clothing and major medical expenses, which are not even included in the Harvard costs cited above. When these items are excluded, the cost of nine months in the Job Corps is only $3100, less than half the cost of nine months at Harvard.

Furthermore, these cost estimates for Job Corps are figured on present enrollment plans and include initial startup expenses. Once the program is in full-scale operation at full strength, these costs could easily drop substantially.

Source: Washington Post, March 21, 1965, E6.

The real test for both a Harvard education and a Job Corps education is not how much it costs, however, but how successful the graduates are. No one doubts that it is worth the cost of a Harvard education to produce outstanding businessmen, top college professors and leading Senators. I think it makes just as good sense to take a boy or girl who was born and raised in poverty and, as a result, faces adult life without the education and training needed to get a job, and provide that education and training through the Job Corps.

The real question for taxpayers to decide is not whether the Job Corps costs more or less than a Harvard education, but whether it is worth investing tax revenues in education and training to keep these young men and women off tomorrow's relief rolls, and out of tomorrow's courts, and get them into tomorrow's ranks of productive citizens and taxpayers. That is what the Job Corps is all about.

SARGENT SHRIVER,
Director, Office of Economic Opportunity.
Washington.

QUESTIONS

1. What broader point is Shriver making about the U.S. economy at this moment in history?
2. Who seems to be the audience for this defense?
3. Why does the author think the Job Corps is worthwhile?

28.3. *PLAYBOY MAGAZINE*, "PLAYBOY INTERVIEW: TIMOTHY LEARY—A CASUAL CONVERSATION" (1966)

In a 1966 *Playboy Magazine* interview, Timothy Leary praised psychedelic drugs for their value in opening new areas of human consciousness. He urged young people to "turn on, tune in, drop out," a phrase that soon became symbolic of the larger counterculture.

PLAYBOY: According to a spokesman for the student left, many former campus activists who've gone the LSD route are "more concerned with what's happening in their heads than what's happening in the world." Any comment?

LEARY: There's a certain amount of truth in that. The insight of LSD leads you to concern yourself more with internal or spiritual values; you realize that it doesn't make any difference what you do on the outside unless you change the inside. If all the Negroes and left-wing college students in the world had Cadillacs and full control of society, they would still be involved in an anthill social system unless they opened themselves up first.

PLAYBOY: Aren't these young ex-activists among an increasing number of students, writers, artists and musicians whom one critic has called "the psychedelic dropouts," LSD users who find themselves divested of motivation, unable to readjust to reality or to resume their roles in society?

LEARY: There is an LSD dropout problem, but it's nothing to worry about. It's something to cheer. The lesson I have learned from over 300 LSD sessions, and which I have been passing on to others,

Source: "Playboy_ Interview:_Timothy_Leary_—A_ Casual_Conversation." _*Playboy*. Sept._1966,_Vol._13,_No._9,_pp._ 93–113.

can be stated in six syllables: Turn on, tune in, drop out. "Turn on" means to contact the ancient energies and wisdoms that are built into your nervous system. They provide unspeakable pleasure and revelation. "Tune in" means to harness and communicate these new perspectives in a harmonious dance with the external world. "Drop out" means to detach yourself from the tribal game. Current models of social adjustment—mechanized, computerized, socialized, intellectualized, televised, Sanforized—make no sense to the new LSD generation, who see clearly that American society is becoming an air-conditioned anthill. In every generation of human history, thoughtful men have turned on and dropped out of the tribal game, and thus stimulated the larger society to lurch ahead. Every historical advance has resulted from the stern pressure of visionary men who have declared their independence from the game: "Sorry, George III, we don't buy your model. We're going to try something new"; "Sorry, Louis XVI, we've got a new idea. Deal us out"; "Sorry, L.B.J., it's time to mosey on beyond the Great Society." The reflex reaction of society to the creative dropout is panic and irritation. If anyone questions the social order, he threatens the whole shaky edifice. The automatic, angry reaction to the creative dropout is that he will become a parasite on the hard-working, conforming citizen. This is not true. The LSD experience does not lead to passivity and withdrawal; it spurs a driving hunger to communicate in new forms, in better ways, to express a more harmonious message, to live a better life. The LSD cult has already wrought revolutionary changes in American culture. If you were to conduct a poll of the creative young musicians in this country, you'd find that at least 80 percent are using psychedelic drugs in a systematic way. And this new psychedelic style has produced not only a new rhythm in modern music but a new decor for our discotheques, a new form of film making, a new kinetic visual art, a new literature, and has begun to revise our philosophic and psychological thinking.

Remember, it's the college kids who are turning on the smartest and most promising of the youngsters. What an exciting prospect: a generation of creative youngsters refusing to march in step, refusing to go to offices, refusing to sign up on the installment plan, refusing to climb aboard the treadmill.

PLAYBOY: What will they do?

LEARY: Don't worry. Each one will work out his individual solution. Some will return to the establishment and inject their new ideas. Some will live underground as self-employed artists, artisans and writers. Some are already forming small communities out of the country. Many are starting schools for children and adults who wish to learn the use of their sense organs. Psychedelic businesses are springing up: bookstores, art galleries. Psychedelic industries may involve more manpower in the future than the automobile industry has produced in the last 20 years. In our technological society of the future, the problem will be not to get people to work, but to develop graceful, fulfilling ways of living a more serene, beautiful and creative life. Psychedelics will help to point the way.

QUESTIONS

1. What is Leary's argument about the importance of drugs?
2. In what ways does he believe that drug use will simply become part of modern life?

28.4. VISUAL DOCUMENT: TIMOTHY LEARY AND ELDRIDGE CLEAVER IN ALGERIAN EXILE (1970)

On October 20, 1970, LSD prophet Dr. Timothy Leary escaped from a jail in San Luis Obispo, California, where he was serving a sentence for a conviction on possession of marijuana. Inmate Leary was a psychologist with a PhD from the University of California–Berkeley and former Harvard lecturer. As a researcher, he was a leading proponent of the therapeutic use of psychedelic drugs. His personal enthusiasm for drugs led to his dismissal from Harvard in 1963. By the time he escaped from jail, he was famous for his mantra, "Tune in, Turn On, Drop Out," and was a leading figure in the counterculture. After escaping from jail, Leary fled the United States, seeking political asylum in Algeria along with his wife Rosemary, joining fellow American refugee, Black Panther party leader Eldridge Cleaver. Cleaver fled the United States after being charged with murder in connection to a California shooting involving the Oakland Police Department.

Larry Mack—International Section—Black Panther Party
Privileged exiles: Eldridge Cleaver and Leary in Algiers

QUESTIONS

1. How might you try to offer some broader historical context for the strange exile relationship of Leary and Cleaver?

2. What do these briefly linked stories say about the cultural upheaval and international character of the 1960s and early 1970s?

Source: Photo by Larry Mack

28.5. VISUAL DOCUMENT: ASSOCIATED PRESS, BLACK POWER PROTEST AT THE 1968 MEXICO CITY OLYMPICS (1968)

At the 1968 Olympic Games in Mexico City, U.S. athletes Tommie Smith (center) and John Carlos (right) raised their fists in the Black Power salute after winning the gold and bronze medals, respectively. Their demonstration led to their expulsion from the games and subsequent ostracism by U.S. track and field officials.

QUESTIONS

1. Why do you think this simple act of protest became an icon of changing views of civil rights?

2. Does the act captured in this photo seem to merit the very strong reaction and punishment? Why do you think officials reacted as they did?

Source: AP Photo/FILE

28.6. CESAR CHAVEZ, SPEECH AT HARVARD UNIVERSITY (1970)

In March 1970, Cesar Chavez, organizer of the four-year-old Delano Grape Strike, tells an audience at Harvard University of the hardships encountered by the men and women who were trying to organize California's farm workers.

You know, we have had a long historical struggle in the fields of California to form unions. Very little has been recorded, very little has been written about it, because in most cases this struggle has been waged by immigrant groups. In many cases those groups made very little achievement, but for the last seven years there have been basic struggles to organize, and for seven years these attempts have been thwarted and broken by the overwhelming power of the employer groups.

Today in Delano we have a group of men and women who have done outstanding work to try and liberate themselves through their collective action to get those things in life that other workers have had so long. They have gone to great expense and personal selfless dedication and work just to stay alive as a group. We ourselves frequently ask: What causes a man to give up his paycheck for forty-eight months—forty-nine months now—however small it may be, for the right to have a living? Or what would cause a woman striker to picket and demonstrate, peacefully and non-violently, and then be arrested as a common criminal? Or what would cause men and women in the struggle to suffer the painful separation from family and be sent across the country to all the major cities and Canada, to bring the word of the boycott and the struggle of the farm workers? We often ask ourselves: What would cause teenage boys and girls to [go to] school without a new pair of shoes or go to school with the same old clothes and do without noon lunch? What causes this greatest personal sacrifice? Why are they going insane?

Or what would cause still little children who are too small to understand the struggle, to do without milk, to do without the basic necessities of life because their parents are involved in what is getting to be perhaps the longest and, perhaps, we hope, the most successful strike of farm workers ever in the history of our country? We say that what causes this is what causes other people in other parts of the world and in our own country—a spirit of independence and freedom, the spirit that they want to change things and that they want to be independent and they want to be able to run their own lives. This is the cause why these workers are so willing to bear the sacrifices and all the personal suffering that go with the strike and boycott.

You know, organizing farm workers is very different from organizing any other workers in the country today. Here we don't have any rules, any regulations. We don't have any prescribed methods, no precedents. There is no law for farm labor organizing, save the law of the jungle. The citizens and their rights for seven years have been ignored and the employers have seen to it that they don't survive. Agriculture in this country is not a family with a small plot of land. That is not agriculture, that is not where the fruits and the vegetables, the nuts and the grapes are produced. They [are] produced in large factory farms, huge corporate farms. They themselves have adopted a new name: they call themselves "agrobusiness."

It is against agro-business, in such combinations as they have going now with the Defense Department, that we have to deal. For we had cut the sales of grapes

Source: Cesar Chavez, An Organizer's Tale: Speeches (New York: Penguin, 2008), 88–90.

nationally thirty percent. The Defense Department, on the other hand, is increasing its purchases to the extent that they are now shipping to Vietnam eight hundred percent more grapes than they were in the beginning of the boycott. . . .

But it is no joke that the Defense Department is in a deal with agro-business for the sole purpose of breaking the strike. And the eight hundred percent only takes us to the end of the last fiscal year. As the report comes from the first quarter of this new fiscal year; we don't know what the percentage may be. We can very well guess that it will probably be about a thousand percent. That means they are sending to Vietnam now about eight pounds of grapes per man. Imagine what happens over there when a fellow doesn't like grapes gets that much!

But in the face of this overwhelming power, enough to wipe out literally any attempt of a group of people to organize, we will continue to work, we will continue to spread our strike and boycott to many parts of the world. We have been able to enlist the support of the transport workers throughout the world, the support of the metal-workers, all the labor movements in Canada and the labor movement here, the church supporting us in a manner to be marvelled at, and the liberal community. But it was not like this always. There was a time at the beginning of the strike when people were afraid of us. There was a time at the beginning of the strike when we stood alone with the workers and when no one dared to come near us. No one dared to come near us because we were being red-baited. And it did not come to be what it is today, except for today, thank God—and we thank them a million times—the students who came to our support right from the beginning. So there is sympathy of the worker in this struggle for students whoever they may be.

QUESTIONS

1. How does Chavez relate his struggle with historic issues?
2. What does Chavez mean when he says that the protestors were being "red-baited"?
3. How does this struggle for workers' rights compare to the privileged student protest goals explained in the documents from Students for a Democratic Society?

CHAPTER 29

CONSERVATISM RESURGENT, 1973 TO 1988

29.1. PHYLLIS SCHLAFLY, "THE POWER OF POSITIVE WOMEN" (1977)

The modern feminist movement of the 1950s and 1960s was not universally endorsed by American women. Phyllis Schlafly, a constitutional lawyer and conservative activist, was an outspoken critic of the women's rights movement and the Equal Rights Amendment. In this passage from her 1977 book, *The Power of Positive Women*, Schlafly challenges the assumptions of the women's rights movement, arguing that the social changes of the 1960s and 1970s were undermining the social and economic status of women.[1]

The first requirement for the acquisition of power by the Positive Woman is to understand the differences between men and women. Your outlook on life, your faith, your behavior, your potential for fulfillment, all are determined by the parameters of your original premise. The Positive Woman starts with the assumption that the world is her oyster. She rejoices in the creative capability within her body and the power potential of her mind and spirit. She understands that men and women are different, and that those very differences provide the key to her success as a person and fulfillment as a woman.

The women's liberationist, on the other hand, is imprisoned by her own negative view of herself and of her place in the world around her. This view of women was most succinctly expressed in an advertisement designed by the principal women's liberationist organization, the National Organization for Women (NOW), and run in many magazines and newspapers and as spot announcements on many television stations. The advertisement showed a darling curlyheaded girl with the caption: "This healthy, normal baby has a handicap. She was born female." . . .

By its very nature, therefore, the women's liberation movement precipitates a series of conflict situations—in the legislatures, in the courts, in the schools, in industry—with man targeted as the enemy. Confrontation replaces cooperation as the watchword

---

1.   Phyllis Schlafly, *The Power of Positive Women* (New Rochelle, NY: Arlington House, 1977), 16–19.

of all relationships. Women and men become adversaries instead of partners. . . .

The women's liberationists and their dupes who try to tell each other that the sexual drive of men and women is really the same, and that it is only societal restraints that inhibit women from an equal desire, an equal enjoyment, and an equal freedom from the consequences, are doomed to frustration forever. It just isn't so, and pretending cannot make it so. The differences are not a woman's weakness but her strength. . . .

The new generation can brag all it wants about the new liberation of the new morality, but it is still the woman who is hurt the most. The new morality isn't just a "fad"—it is a cheat and a thief. It robs the woman of her virtue, her youth, her beauty, and her love—for nothing, just nothing. It has produced a generation of young women searching for their identity, bored with sexual freedom, and despondent from the loneliness of living a life without commitment. They have abandoned the old commandments, but they can't find any new rules that work.

The Positive Woman recognizes the fact that, when it comes to sex, women are simply not the equal of men. The sexual drive of men is much stronger than that of women. That is how the human race was designed in order that it might perpetuate itself. The other side of the coin is that it is easier for women to control their sexual appetites. A Positive Woman cannot defeat a man in a wrestling or boxing match, but she can motivate him, inspire him, encourage him, teach him, restrain him, reward him, and have power over him that he can never achieve over her with all his muscle. How or whether a Positive Woman uses her power is determined solely by the way she alone defines her goals and develops her skills.

The differences between men and women are also emotional and psychological. Without woman's innate maternal instinct, the human race would have died out centuries ago. There is nothing so helpless in all earthly life as the newborn infant. It will die within hours if not cared for. Even in the most primitive, uneducated societies, women have always cared for their newborn babies. They didn't need any schooling to teach them how. They didn't need any welfare workers to tell them it is their social obligation. Even in societies to whom such concepts as "ought," "social responsibility," and

"compassion for the helpless" were unknown, mothers cared for their new babies.

Why? Because caring for a baby serves the natural maternal need of a woman. Although not nearly so total as the baby's need, the woman's need is nonetheless real.

The overriding psychological need of a woman is to love something alive. A baby fulfills this need in the lives of most women. If a baby is not available to fill that need, women search for a baby-substitute. This is the reason why women have traditionally gone into teaching and nursing careers. They are doing what comes naturally to the female psyche. The school-child or the patient of any age provides an outlet for a woman to express her natural maternal need.

This maternal need in women is the reason why mothers whose children have grown up and flown from the nest are sometimes cut loose from their psychological moorings. The maternal need in women can show itself in love for grandchildren, nieces, nephews, or even neighbors' children. The maternal need in some women has even manifested itself in an extraordinary affection lavished on a dog, a cat, or a parakeet.

This is not to say that every woman must have a baby in order to be fulfilled. But it is to say that fulfillment for most women involves expressing their natural maternal urge by loving and caring for someone.

The women's liberation movement complains that traditional stereotyped roles assume that women are "passive" and that men are "aggressive." The anomaly is that a woman's most fundamental emotional need is not passive at all, but active. A woman naturally seeks to love affirmatively and to show that love in an active way by caring for the object of her affections.

The Positive Woman finds somebody on whom she can lavish her maternal love so that it doesn't well up inside her and cause psychological frustrations. Surely no woman is so isolated by geography or insulated by spirit that she cannot find someone worthy of her maternal love. All persons, men and women, gain by sharing something of themselves with their fellow humans, but women profit most of all because it is part of their very nature. . . .

Most women's organizations, recognizing the preference of most women to avoid hard-driving competition, handle the matter of succession of officers by the device of a nominating committee. This eliminates the unpleasantness and the tension of a competitive confrontation every year or two. Many women's organizations customarily use a prayer attributed to Mary, Queen of Scots, which is an excellent analysis by a woman of women's faults:

> Keep us, O God, from pettiness; let us be large in thought, in word, in deed. Let us be done with fault-finding and leave off self-seeking. . . . Grant that we may realize it is the little things that create differences, that in the big things of life we are at one. . . .

Finally, women are different from men in dealing with the fundamentals of life itself. Men are philosophers, women are practical, and 'twas ever thus. Men may philosophize about how life began and where we are heading; women are concerned about feeding the kids today. No woman would ever, as Karl Marx did,

spend years reading political philosophy in the British Museum while her child starved to death. Women don't take naturally to a search for the intangible and the abstract. The Positive Woman knows who she is and where she is going, and she will reach her goal because the longest journey starts with a very practical first step.

QUESTIONS

1. How did Phyllis Schlafly define a "positive woman?" How did positive women differ from "women's liberationists?"
2. What are the differences between men and women? How did the "New Morality" cheat women?
3. How might a women's liberationist respond to Schlafly's arguments?

29.2. JIMMY CARTER, "A CRISIS OF THE AMERICAN SPIRIT" (1979)

After eleven days of dialogue and contemplation at the presidential retreat Camp David, President Jimmy Carter addressed the nation on television the evening of July 15, 1979. With unusual candor for an American politician, the president laid out what he called the national "crisis of confidence" that had developed in the midst of energy and economic problems in the years after the Vietnam War. Carter's address became known as the "malaise" speech, even though he did not use the word. The address would be remembered as another unpopular act of a supposedly failed president, even though the national audience responded positively to it.

I know, of course, being President, that government actions and legislation can be very important. That's why I've worked hard to put my campaign promises into law–and I have to admit, with just mixed success. But after listening to the American people I have been reminded again that all the legislation in the world can't fix what's wrong with America. So, I want to

speak to you first tonight about a subject even more serious than energy or inflation. I want to talk to you right now about a fundamental threat to American democracy.

I do not mean our political and civil liberties. They will endure. And I do not refer to the outward strength of America, a nation that is at peace tonight

Source: Jimmy Carter, "Address to the Nation on Energy and National Goals: 'The Malaise Speech,'" July 15, 1979.

everywhere in the world, with unmatched economic power and military might.

The threat is nearly invisible in ordinary ways. It is a crisis of confidence. It is a crisis that strikes at the very heart and soul and spirit of our national will. We can see this crisis in the growing doubt about the meaning of our own lives and in the loss of a unity of purpose for our Nation.

The erosion of our confidence in the future is threatening to destroy the social and the political fabric of America.

The confidence that we have always had as a people is not simply some romantic dream or a proverb in a dusty book that we readjust on the Fourth of July. It is the idea which founded our Nation and has guided our development as a people. Confidence in the future has supported everything else—public institutions and private enterprise, our own families, and the very Constitution of the United States. Confidence has defined our course and has served as a link between generations. We've always believed in something called progress. We've always had a faith that the days of our children would be better than our own.

Our people are losing that faith, not only in government itself but in the ability as citizens to serve as the ultimate rulers and shapers of our democracy. As a people we know our past and we are proud of it. Our progress has been part of the living history of America, even the world. We always believed that we were part of a great movement of humanity itself called democracy, involved in the search for freedom, and that belief has always strengthened us in our purpose. But just as we are losing our confidence in the future, we are also beginning to close the door on our past.

In a nation that was proud of hard work, strong families, close-knit communities, and our faith in God, too many of us now tend to worship self-indulgence and consumption. Human identity is no longer defined by what one does, but by what one owns. But we've discovered that owning things and consuming things does not satisfy our longing for meaning. We've learned that piling up material goods cannot fill the emptiness of lives which have no confidence or purpose.

The symptoms of this crisis of the American spirit are all around us. For the first time in the history of our country a majority of our people believe that the next 5 years will be worse than the past 5 years. Two-thirds of our people do not even vote. The productivity of American workers is actually dropping, and the willingness of Americans to save for the future has fallen below that of all other people in the Western world.

As you know, there is a growing disrespect for government and for churches and for schools, the news media, and other institutions. This is not a message of happiness or reassurance, but it is the truth and it is a warning.

These changes did not happen overnight. They've come upon us gradually over the last generation, years that were filled with shocks and tragedy.

We were sure that ours was a nation of the ballot, not the bullet, until the murders of John Kennedy and Robert Kennedy and Martin Luther King, Jr. We were taught that our armies were always invincible and our causes were always just, only to suffer the agony of Vietnam. We respected the Presidency as a place of honor until the shock of Watergate.

We remember when the phrase "sound as a dollar" was an expression of absolute dependability, until 10 years of inflation began to shrink our dollar and our savings. We believed that our Nation's resources were limitless until 1973, when we had to face a growing dependence on foreign oil.

These wounds are still very deep. They have never been healed.

Looking for a way out of this crisis, our people have turned to the Federal Government and found it isolated from the mainstream of our Nation's life. Washington, D.C., has become an island. The gap between our citizens and our Government has never been so wide. The people are looking for honest answers, not easy answers; clear leadership, not false claims and evasiveness and politics as usual.

What you see too often in Washington and elsewhere around the country is a system of government that seems incapable of action. You see a Congress twisted and pulled in every direction by hundreds of well-financed and powerful special interests. You see every extreme position defended to the last vote, almost to the last breath by one unyielding group or another. You often see a balanced and a fair approach that demands sacrifice, a little sacrifice from everyone, abandoned like an orphan without support and without friends.

Often you see paralysis and stagnation and drift. You don't like it, and neither do I. What can we do?

First of all, we must face the truth, and then we can change our course. We simply must have faith in each other, faith in our ability to govern ourselves, and faith in the future of this Nation. Restoring that faith and that confidence to America is now the most important task we face. It is a true challenge of this generation of Americans.

One of the visitors to Camp David last week put it this way: "We've got to stop crying and start sweating, stop talking and start walking, stop cursing and start praying. The strength we need will not come from the White House, but from every house in America."

We know the strength of America. We are strong. We can regain our unity. We can regain our confidence. We are the heirs of generations who survived threats much more powerful and awesome than those that challenge us now. Our fathers and mothers were strong men and women who shaped a new society during the Great Depression, who fought world wars, and who carved out a new charter of peace for the world.

We ourselves are the same Americans who just 10 years ago put a man on the Moon. We are the generation that dedicated our society to the pursuit of human rights and equality. And we are the generation that will win the war on the energy problem and in that process rebuild the unity and confidence of America.

We are at a turning point in our history. There are two paths to choose. One is a path I've warned about tonight, the path that leads to fragmentation and self-interest. Down that road lies a mistaken idea of freedom, the right to grasp for ourselves some advantage over others. That path would be one of constant conflict between narrow interests ending in chaos and immobility. It is a certain route to failure.

All the traditions of our past, all the lessons of our heritage, all the promises of our future point to another path, the path of common purpose and the restoration of American values. That path leads to true freedom for our Nation and ourselves. We can take the first steps down that path as we begin to solve our energy problem.

QUESTIONS

1. What was the nature of the "crisis" among Americans that Carter referred to in his speech?
2. What were some examples the president cited about how this crisis had impacted ordinary people?
3. How did Carter propose that people and government work to solve this set of problems?

29.3. JERRY FALWELL, "LISTEN, AMERICA" (1981)

Although many Americans embraced the cultural and social revolutions of the 1960s and 1970s, many others feared that the apparent collapse of traditional moral values threatened the nation's future. Jerry Falwell (1933–2007), a Southern Baptist pastor and fundamentalist televangelist, helped mobilize critics of social change by founding the Moral Majority in 1979. The Moral Majority opposed the Equal Rights Amendment, abortion, school busing, and civil rights for homosexuals and supported capital punishment, school prayer, lower taxes, and smaller government. In this passage, Falwell encourages fundamentalist Christians and other social conservatives to organize for political action.

Listen, America! Our nation is on a perilous path in regard to her political, economic, and military positions. If America continues down the path she is traveling, she will one day find that she is no longer a free nation. Our nation's internal problems are direct results of her spiritual condition. America is desperately in need of a divine healing, which can only come if God's people will humble themselves, pray, seek His face, and turn from their wicked ways. It is now time that moral Americans awake to the fact that our future depends upon how we stand on moral issues. God has no reason to spare us if we continue to reject Him.

America has been great because her people have been good. We are certainly far from being a perfect society, but our heritage is one of genuine concern for all mankind. It is God Almighty who has made and preserved us as a nation, and the day that we forget that is the day that the United States will become a byword among the nations of the world. We will become nothing more than a memory in a history book, like the many great civilizations that have preceded us. America's only hope for survival is a spiritual awakening that begins in the lives of her individual citizens. It is only in the spiritual rebirth of our nation's citizens that we can have a positive hope in the future. The destiny of America awaits that decision. . . .

Bible-believing Christians and concerned moral Americans are determined to do something about the problems that we are facing as a nation. . . .

My responsibility as a parent-pastor is more than just concern. The issue of convenience is not even up for discussion. If the moral issues are really matters of conviction that are worth living for, then they are worth fighting for. In discussing these matters further with other pastors and concerned Christian leaders, I have become convinced of the need to have a coalition of God-fearing, moral Americans to represent our convictions to our government. I realize that there would be those pastors who misunderstand our intentions. I know that some object that we are compromising in our involvement with people of different doctrinal and theological beliefs. As a fundamental, independent, separatist Baptist, I am well aware of the crucial issues of personal and ecclesiastical separation that divide fundamentalists philosophically from evangelicals and liberals. I do not believe that it is ever right to compromise the truth in order to gain an opportunity to do right. In doctrinal and spiritual matters, there is no real harmony between light and darkness.

I am convinced of two very significant factors. First, our very moral existence as a nation is at stake. There are many moral Americans who do not share our theological beliefs but who do share our moral concerns. Second, we must face the fact that it will take the greatest possible number of concerned citizens to reverse the politicization of immorality in our society. Doctrinal difference is a distinctive feature of a democracy. Our freedoms have given us the privilege and the

Source: Jerry Falwell, *Listen, America!* (New York: Doubleday, 1980), 213, 224–34.

luxury of theological disagreement. I would not for a moment encourage anyone to water down his distinctive beliefs. But we must face realistically the fact that there are Christians in the world today who have lost the luxury of disagreement. When the entire issue of Christian survival is at stake, we must be willing to band together on at least the major moral issues of the day. . . .

Our ministry is as committed as it ever has been to the basic truths of Scripture, to essential and fundamental Christian doctrines. But we are not willing to isolate ourselves in seclusion while we sit back and watch this nation plunge headlong toward hell. . . .

To change America we must be involved, and this includes three areas of political action:

1. REGISTRATION

A recent national poll indicated that eight million American evangelicals are not registered to vote. I am convinced that this is one of the major sins of the church today. Until concerned Christian citizens become registered voters there is very little that we can do to change the tide of political influence on the social issues in our nation. Those who object to Christians being involved in the political process are ultimately objecting to Christians being involved in the social process. The political process is really nothing more than a realization of the social process. For us to divorce ourselves from society would be to run into the kind of isolationism and monasticism that characterized the medieval hermits. Many Christians are not even aware of the importance of registering to vote. It is perfectly legal, for example, for a deputy registrar to come right to your local church at a designated time and register the entire congregation. I am convinced that those of us who are pastors have an obligation to urge our people to register to vote. I am more concerned that people exercise their freedom to vote than I am concerned for whom they vote.

2. INFORMATION

Many moral Americans are unaware of the real issues affecting them today. Many people do not know the voting record of their congressman and have no idea how he is representing them on political issues that have moral implications. This is one of the major reasons why we have established the Moral Majority organization. We want to keep the public informed on the vital moral issues. The Moral Majority, Inc., is a nonprofit organization, with headquarters in Washington, D.C. Our goal is to exert a significant influence on the spiritual and moral direction of our nation by: (a) mobilizing the grassroots of moral Americans in one clear and effective voice; (b) informing the moral majority what is going on behind their backs in Washington and in state legislatures across the country; (c) lobbying intensely in Congress to defeat left-wing, social-welfare bills that will further erode our precious freedom; (d) pushing for positive legislation such as that to establish the Family Protection Agency, which will ensure a strong, enduring America; and (e) helping the moral majority in local communities to fight pornography, homosexuality, the advocacy of immorality in school textbooks, and other issues facing each and every one of us.

Christians must keep America great by being willing to go into the halls of Congress, by getting laws passed that will protect the freedom and liberty of her citizens. The Moral Majority, Inc., was formed to acquaint Americans everywhere with the tragic decline in our nation's morals and to provide leadership in establishing an effective coalition of morally active citizens who are (a) prolife, (b) profamily, (c) promoral, and (d) pro-American. If the vast majority of Americans (84 percent, according to George Gallup) still believe the Ten Commandments are valid today, why are we permitting a few leading amoral humanists and naturalists to take over the most influential positions in this nation? . . .

3. MOBILIZATION

The history of the church includes the history of Christian involvement in social issues. . . .

The turning point in Christian involvement in social action seems to have been the repeal of prohibition in 1933. A wide variety of Christians and moral Americans were united in the crusade against alcohol for nearly twenty years. Led by the preaching of evangelist Billy Sunday, prohibition finally became law in

1919. Its eventual repeal caused many Christians to conclude that we have no business trying to legislate Christian morality on a non-Christian society. The Depression and World War II followed shortly thereafter, and Christian concern about social issues hit rock bottom during the fifties and sixties. We have tended to develop the attitude that our only obligation is to preach the Gospel and prepare men for heaven. We have forgotten that we are still our brother's keeper and that the same spiritual truths that prepare us to live in eternity are also essential in preparing us to live on this earth. We dare not advocate our responsibility to the society of which we are so very much a vital part. If we as moral Americans do not speak up on these essential moral issues, who then will? As Christians we need to exert our influence not only in the church but also in our business life, home life, and social and community life as well. . . .

Right living must be re-established as an American way of life. We as American citizens must recommit ourselves to the faith of our fathers and to the premises and moral foundations upon which this country was established. Now is the time to begin calling America back to God, back to the Bible, back to morality! We must be willing to live by the moral convictions that we claim to believe. There is no way that we will ever be willing to die for something for which we are not willing to live. The authority of Bible morality must once again be recognized as the legitimate guiding principle of our nation. Our love for our fellow man must ever be grounded in the truth and never be allowed to blind us from the truth that is the basis of our love for our fellow man.

As a pastor and as a parent I am calling my fellow American citizens to unite in a moral crusade for righteousness in our generation, it is time to call America back to her moral roots. It is time to call America back to God. We need a revival of righteous living based on a proper confession of sin and repentance of heart if we are to remain the land of the free and the home of the brave! I am convinced that God is calling millions of Americans in the so-often silent majority to join in the moral-majority crusade to turn America around in our lifetime. Won't you begin now to pray with us for revival in America? Let us unite our hearts and lives together for the cause of a new America . . . a moral America in which righteousness will exalt this nation. Only as we do this can we exempt ourselves from one day having to look our children in the eyes and answer this searching question: "Mom and Dad, where were you the day freedom died in America?"

The choice is now ours.

QUESTIONS

1. According to Jerry Falwell, why did "Bible-believing Christians" need to become politically active in the 1980s?
2. What was the purpose of the Moral Majority? What issues did it address? How was it organized?
3. What sort of action did Falwell favor?

29.4. RONALD REAGAN, "SPEECH TO THE NATIONAL ASSOCIATION OF EVANGELICALS" (1983)

Reagan's speech to the National Association of Evangelicals in March 1983 provided him with the opportunity to link his strident anticommunism and evangelical faith to social issues such as his opposition to abortion, high taxes, and "activist" federal judges. Government policies, he argued, must be consistent with precepts contained in the Bible.

I want you to know that this administration is motivated by a political philosophy that sees the greatness of America in you, her people, and in your families, churches, neighborhoods, communities—the institutions that foster and nourish values like concern for others and respect for the rule of law under God.

Now, I don't have to tell you that this puts us in opposition to, or at least out of step with, a prevailing attitude of many who have turned to a modern-day secularism, discarding the tried and time-tested values upon which our very civilization is based. No matter how well intentioned, their value system is radically different from that of most Americans. And while they proclaim that they're freeing us from superstitions of the past, they've taken upon themselves the job of superintending us by government rule and regulation. Sometimes their voices are louder than ours, but they are not yet a majority. . . .

Let me state the case as briefly and simply as I can. An organization of citizens, sincerely motivated and deeply concerned about the increase in illegitimate births and abortions involving girls well below the age of consent, some time ago established a nationwide network of clinics to offer help to these girls and, hopefully, alleviate this situation. Now, again, let me say, I do not fault their intent. However, in their well-intentioned effort, these clinics have decided to provide advice and birth control drugs and devices to underage girls without the knowledge of their parents. . . .

Is all of Judeo-Christian tradition wrong? Are we to believe that something so sacred can be looked upon as a purely physical thing with no potential for emotional and psychological harm? And isn't it the parents' right to give counsel and advice to keep their children from making mistakes that may affect their entire lives? . . .

More than a decade ago, a Supreme Court decision literally wiped off the books of 50 States statutes protecting the rights of unborn children. Abortion on demand now takes the lives of up to 1½ million unborn children a year. Human life legislation ending this tragedy will some day pass the Congress, and you and I must never rest until it does. Unless and until it can be proven that the unborn child is not a living entity, then its right to life, liberty, and the pursuit of happiness must be protected.

You may remember that when abortion on demand began, many, and, indeed, I'm sure many of you, warned that the practice would lead to a decline in respect for human life, that the philosophical premises used to justify abortion on demand would ultimately be used to justify other attacks on the sacredness of human life—infanticide or mercy killing. Tragically enough, those warnings proved all too true. Only last year a court permitted the death by starvation of a handicapped infant. . . .

Recent legislation introduced in the Congress by Representative Henry Hyde of Illinois not only increases restrictions on publicly financed abortions, it also addresses this whole problem of infanticide. I

Source: *Congressional Record*, March 1983.

urge the Congress to begin hearings and to adopt legislation that will protect the right of life to all children, including the disabled or handicapped.

Now, I'm sure that you must get discouraged at times, but you've done better than you know, perhaps. There's a great spiritual awakening in America, a renewal of the traditional values that have been the bedrock of America's goodness and greatness.

One recent survey by a Washington-based research council concluded that Americans were far more religious than the people of other nations; 95 percent of those surveyed expressed a belief in God and a huge majority believed the Ten Commandments had real meaning in their lives. And another study has found that an overwhelming majority of Americans disapprove of adultery, teenage sex, pornography, abortion, and hard drugs. And this same study showed a deep reverence for the importance of family ties and religious belief.

I think the items that we've discussed here today must be a key part of the Nation's political agenda. For the first time the Congress is openly and seriously debating and dealing with the prayer and abortion issues—and that's enormous progress right there. I repeat: America is in the midst of a spiritual awakening and a moral renewal. And with your Biblical keynote, I say today, "Yes, let justice roll on like a river, righteousness like a never-failing stream." . . .

And this brings me to my final point today. During my first press conference as President, in answer to a direct question, I pointed out that, as good Marxist-Leninists, the Soviet leaders have openly and publicly declared that the only morality they recognize is that which will further their cause, which is world revolution. I think I should point out I was only quoting Lenin, their guiding spirit, who said in 1920 that they repudiate all morality that proceeds from supernatural ideas—that's their name for religion—or ideas that are outside class conceptions. Morality is entirely subordinate to the interests of class war. And everything is moral that is necessary for the annihilation of the old. . . .

They must be made to understand we will never compromise our principles and standards. We will never give away our freedom. We will never abandon our belief in God. And we will never stop searching for a genuine peace. But we can assure none of these things America stands for through the so-called nuclear freeze solutions proposed by some. . . .

Yes, let us pray for the salvation of all of those who live in that totalitarian darkness—pray they will discover the joy of knowing God. But until they do, let us be aware that while they preach the supremacy of the state, declare its omnipotence over individual man, and predict its eventual domination of all peoples on the Earth, they are the focus of evil in the modern world. . . .

I believe we shall rise to the challenge. I believe that communism is another sad, bizarre chapter in human history whose last pages even now are being written. I believe this because the source of our strength in the quest for human freedom is not material, but spiritual. And because it knows no limitation, it must terrify and ultimately triumph over those who would enslave their fellow man.

QUESTIONS

1. What specific evils did Reagan associate with communism?
2. Why did Reagan believe that religious faith was an antidote to communism?

29.5. VISUAL DOCUMENT: *RONBO*

As a candidate for president and throughout his first term, Reagan spoke in strident tones about the communist threat, the need to rearm America, and his determination to roll back Soviet influence in the Third World. His unapologetic, muscular patriotism showed in White House photographs and in his fans' identification of him with the action hero "Rambo." Reagan's supporters projected an image of his muscular power, building on the theme of the popular Rambo films.

QUESTIONS

1. How did Reagan use imagery to appeal to patriotic sentiment?

2. How did his supporters use popular culture to boost his Superman image?

CHAPTER 30

AFTER THE COLD WAR, 1988 TO 2001

30.1. ROBERT REICH, *THE WORK OF NATIONS* (1991)

By the 1990s, the globalization of manufacturing shifted well-paying industrial jobs from the United States and other developed countries to developing countries in Asia and South America. The loss of manufacturing jobs was somewhat mitigated by the expansion of the service sector and the growing influence of "symbolic analysts," but service jobs did not pay as well as the old factory jobs, and becoming a symbolic analyst required obtaining an expensive education. The result was a dramatic redistribution of wealth in the United States. Robert Reich, a political economist at Harvard University and future secretary of labor in the Clinton administration, documented the growing economic gap between the poorest and wealthiest Americans in *The Work of Nations*, an early study of the consequences of globalization.

A summary is in order. My argument thus far is that the economic well-being of Americans (or, for that matter, of any other group of people sharing a common political identity) no longer depends on the profitability of the corporations they own, or on the prowess of their industries, but on the value they add to the global economy through their skills and insights. Increasingly, it is the jobs that Americans do, rather than the success of abstract entities like corporations, industries, or national economies, that determine their standard of living. . . .

Data on the distribution of American incomes are not free from controversy. Like any data, they can be interpreted in slightly different ways, depending on the weights accorded a host of other changes that have occurred simultaneously, and also depending on which years are selected for measurement and how the measurements are done. But nearly everyone agrees that the trend, at least since the mid-1970s, has been toward inequality.

Controlling for family size, geography, and other changes, the best estimate—which I cited earlier—is that between 1977 and 1990 the average income of the poorest fifth of Americans declined by about 5 percent, while the richest fifth became about 9 percent wealthier. During these years, the average incomes of the poorest fifth of American *families* declined by about 7 percent, while the average income of the richest fifth of American families increased about 15 percent. That left the poorest fifth of Americans by 1990 with 3.7

Source: Robert Reich, *The Work of Nations* (New York: Alfred A. Knopf, 1991), 196–98, 202–4, 208–21.

percent of the nation's total income, down from 5.5 percent twenty years before—the lowest portion they have received since 1954. And it left the richest fifth with a bit over half of the nation's income—the highest portion ever recorded by the top 20 percent. The top 5 percent commanded 26 percent of the nation's total income, another record.

Picture a symmetrical wave that's highest in the middle and then gradually slopes down and out on both ends until merging with the horizon. Through the 1950s and 1960s, the distribution of income in the United States was coming to resemble just this sort of a wave. Most Americans were bunching up in the middle of the wave, enjoying medium incomes. Fewer Americans were on the sides, either very poor or very rich. Only a tiny minority were at the outermost edges, extremely poor or extremely rich. But beginning in the mid-1970s, and accelerating sharply in the 1980s, the crest of the wave began to move toward the poorer end. More Americans were poor. The middle began to sag, as the portion of middle-income Americans dropped. And the end representing the richest Americans began to elongate, as the rich became much, much richer.

The trend should not be overstated. Some researchers, selecting different years and using different measurements, have found the divergence to be somewhat less pronounced. But overall, the trend is unmistakable. There is good reason to suspect that it is not a temporary aberration, and that the gap will, if anything, grow wider. . . .

Even taken together, the conventional explanations for the widening gap between rich and poor account for only part of the answer. Interestingly, several other advanced economies—with different tax and welfare policies than the United States, and different demographic swings—have experienced a similar shift toward inequality. That the gap widened noticeably in Margaret Thatcher's Britain is perhaps no surprise, but even the benevolent social-democratic Netherlands has not been immune to the trend. A wide divergence between the incomes of a few at the top and almost everyone else has long been a seemingly immutable feature of life in many underdeveloped economies of course but the trend there has a new feature. Today's Third World elites are less likely to be descended from generations of wealthy landholders more likely to have gained their wealth from the jobs they do. After the land redistribution of the 1950s, for example, Taiwan became one of the world's most egalitarian societies. But, while income is still more evenly distributed there than in most developing nations, the gap between rich and poor widened considerably during the 1980s. The streets of Taipei are now clogged with Mercedes-Benzes, Volvos, and Jaguars, as well as rickety bicycles.

One important clue: The growth in inequality within the United States (as well as in many other nations) has been dramatic even among people who already hold jobs. Recall that through most of the postwar era, at least until the mid-1970s, the wages of Americans at different income levels rose at about the same pace—roughly 2.5 to 3 percent a year. Meanwhile, the wage gap between workers at the top and those at the bottom steadily narrowed—in part, because of the benign influence of America's core corporations and labor unions in raising the bottom and constraining the top.

In those days, poverty was a consequence of not having a job. The major postwar economic challenge was to create enough jobs for all Americans able to work. Full employment was the battle cry of American liberals, arrayed against conservatives who worried about the inflationary tendencies of a full-employment economy.

Unemployment is now less of a problem, however. In the 1970s and 1980s, over 25 million new jobs were created in the United States, 18.2 million of them in the 1980s alone. There is often a mismatch between where the jobs are and where the people are, of course. Many suburban fast-food jobs go unfilled while inner-city kids cannot easily commute to them. And the Federal Reserve Board periodically cools the economy in an effort to fight inflation, thus drafting into the inflation fight many thousands of those Americans who can least afford it. But these impediments notwithstanding, the truth is that by the last decade of the twentieth century, almost all Americans who wanted to work could find a job. And because population growth has been slowing (more on this later), the demand for people to fill jobs is likely to be higher still in years to come. State governors and city mayors continue to worry every time a factory closes and to congratulate themselves every time they lure new jobs to their jurisdictions. Yet the more important issue over the longer term is the *quality* of jobs, not the number.

By the 1990s, many jobs failed to provide a living wage. More than half of the 32.5 million Americans whose incomes fell under the official poverty line—and nearly two-thirds of all poor children—lived in households with at least one worker. This is a much higher rate of working poor than at any other time in the postwar era. The number of impoverished working Americans climbed by nearly 2 million, or 23 percent, between 1978 and 1987 (years at similar points in the business cycle). Among full-time, year-round workers, the number who were poor climbed even more sharply—by 43 percent. In fact, two-parent families with a full-time worker fell further below the poverty line, on average, than any other type of family, including single parents on welfare.

The wage gap has been widening even within the core American corporation (or, more precisely, that portion of the global web that is formally owned and managed by Americans). By 1990, the average hourly earnings of American non-supervisory workers within American-owned corporations, adjusted for inflation, were lower than in any year since 1965. Middle-level managers fared somewhat better, although their median earnings (adjusted for inflation) were only slightly above the levels of the 1970s.

But between 1977 and 1990, top executives of American-owned corporations reaped a bonanza. Their average remuneration rose by 220 percent, or about 12 percent a year, compounded. (This is aside from the standard perquisites of company car, company plane, country club membership, estate planning, physical examinations, and so forth.) . . .

Regardless of how your job is officially classified (manufacturing, service, managerial, technical, secretarial, and so on), or the industry in which you work (automotive, steel, computer, advertising, finance, food processing), your real competitive position in the world economy is coming to depend on the function you perform in it. Herein lies the basic reason why incomes are diverging. The fortunes of routine producers are declining. In-person servers are also becoming poorer, although their fates are less clear-cut. But symbolic analysts—who solve, identify, and broker new problems—are, by and large, succeeding in the world economy.

All Americans used to be in roughly the same economic boat. Most rose or fell together, as the corporations in which they were employed, the industries comprising such corporations, and the national economy as a whole became more productive—or languished. But national borders no longer define our economic fates. We are now in different boats, one sinking rapidly, one sinking more slowly, and the third rising steadily.

The boat containing routine producers is sinking rapidly. Recall that by midcentury routine production workers in the United States were paid relatively well. The giant pyramidlike organizations at the core of each major industry coordinated their prices and investments—avoiding the harsh winds of competition and thus maintaining healthy earnings. Some of these earnings, in turn, were reinvested in new plant and equipment (yielding ever-larger-scale economies); another portion went to top managers and investors. But a large and increasing portion went to middle managers and production workers. Work stoppages posed such a threat to high-volume production that organized labor was able to exact an ever-larger premium for its cooperation. And the pattern of wages established within the core corporations influenced the pattern throughout the national economy. Thus the growth of a relatively affluent middle class, able to purchase all the wondrous things produced in high volume by the core corporations.

But, as has been observed, the core is rapidly breaking down into global webs which earn their largest profits from clever problem-solving, -identifying, and brokering. As the costs of transporting standard things and of communicating information about them continue to drop, profit margins on high-volume, standardized production are thinning, because there are few barriers to entry. Modern factories and state-of-the-art machinery can be installed almost anywhere on the globe. Routine producers in the United States, then, are in direct competition with millions of routine producers in other nations. Twelve thousand people are added to the world's population every hour, most of whom, eventually, will happily work for a small fraction of the wages of routine producers in America.

The consequence is clearest in older, heavy industries, where high-volume, standardized production continues its ineluctable move to where labor is cheapest and most accessible around the world. Thus, for example, the Maquiladora factories cluttered along the Mexican side of the U.S. border in the sprawling shanty towns of Tijuana, Mexicali, Nogales, Agua Prieta, and Ciudad Juarez—factories owned mostly by Americans, but increasingly by Japanese—in which more than a half million routine producers assemble parts into finished goods to be shipped into the United States. . . .

This shift of routine production jobs from advanced to developing nations is a great boon to many workers in such nations who otherwise would be jobless or working for much lower wages. These workers, in turn, now have more money with which to purchase symbolic-analytic services from advanced nations (often embedded within all sorts of complex products). The trend is also beneficial to everyone around the world who can now obtain high-volume, standardized products (including information and software) more cheaply than before.

But these benefits do not come without certain costs. In particular the burden is borne by those who no longer have good-paying routine production jobs within advanced economies like the United States. Many of these people used to belong to unions or at least benefited from prevailing wage rates established in collective bargaining agreements. But as the old corporate bureaucracies have flattened into global webs, bargaining leverage has been lost. Indeed, the tacit national bargain is no more.

Overall, the decline in routine jobs has hurt men more than women. This is because the routine production jobs held by men in high-volume metal-bending manufacturing industries had paid higher wages than the routine production jobs held by women in textiles and data processing. As both sets of jobs have been lost, American women in routine production have gained more equal footing with American men—equally poor footing, that is. This is a major reason why the gender gap between male and female wages began to close during the 1980s.

The second of the three boats, carrying in-person servers, is sinking as well, but somewhat more slowly and unevenly. Most in-person servers are paid at or just slightly above the minimum wage and many work only part-time, with the result that their take-home pay is modest, to say the least. Nor do they typically receive all the benefits (health care, life insurance, disability, and so forth) garnered by routine producers in large manufacturing corporations or by symbolic analysts affiliated with the more affluent threads of global webs. In-person servers are sheltered from the direct effects of global competition and, like everyone else, benefit from access to lower-cost products from around the world. But they are not immune to its indirect effects.

For one thing, in-person servers increasingly compete with former routine production workers, who, no longer able to find well-paying routine production jobs, have few alternatives but to seek in-person service jobs. The Bureau of Labor Statistics estimates that of the 2.8 million manufacturing workers who lost their jobs during the early 1980s, fully one-third were rehired in service jobs paying at least 20 percent less.[1] In-person servers must also compete with high school graduates and dropouts who years before had moved easily into routine production jobs but no longer can. And if demographic predictions about the American work force in the first decades of the twenty-first century are correct (and they are likely to be, since most of the people who will comprise the work force are already identifiable), most new entrants into the job market will be black or Hispanic men, or women—groups that in years past have possessed relatively weak technical skills. This will result in an even larger number of people crowding into in-person services. Finally, in-person servers will be competing with growing numbers of immigrants, both legal and illegal, for whom in-person services will comprise the most accessible jobs. (It is estimated that between the mid-1980s and the end of the century, about a quarter of all workers entering the American labor force will be immigrants.[2])

1. U.S. Department of Labor, Bureau of Labor Statistics, "Reemployment Increases among Displaced Workers," October 14, 1986.
2. Federal Immigration and Naturalization Service, *Statistical Yearbook* (Washington, DC: U.S. Government Printing Office, 1986, 1987).

Perhaps the fiercest competition that in-person servers face comes from labor-saving machinery (much of it invented, designed, fabricated, or assembled in other nations, of course). Automated tellers, computerized cashiers, automatic car washes, robotized vending machines, self-service gasoline pumps, and all similar gadgets substitute for the human beings that customers once encountered. Even telephone operators are fast disappearing, as electronic sensors and voice simulators become capable of carrying on conversations that are reasonably intelligent, and always polite. Retail sales workers—among the largest groups of in-person servers—are similarly imperiled. Through personal computers linked to television screens, tomorrow's consumers will be able to buy furniture, appliances, and all sorts of electronic toys from their living rooms—examining the merchandise from all angles, selecting whatever color, size, special features, and price seem most appealing, and then transmitting the order instantly to warehouses from which the selections will be shipped directly to their homes. So, too, with financial transactions, airline and hotel reservations, rental car agreements, and similar contracts, which will be executed between consumers in their homes and computer banks somewhere else on the globe. . . .

Unlike the boats of routine producers and in-person servers, however, the vessel containing America's symbolic analysts is rising. Worldwide demand for their insights is growing as the ease and speed of communicating them steadily increases. Not every symbolic analyst is rising as quickly or as dramatically as every other, of course; symbolic analysts at the low end are barely holding their own in the world economy. But symbolic analysts at the top are in such great demand worldwide that they have difficulty keeping track of all their earnings. Never before in history has opulence on such a scale been gained by people who have earned it, and done so legally.

Among symbolic analysts in the middle range are American scientists and researchers who are busily selling their discoveries to global enterprise webs. They are not limited to American customers. If the strategic brokers in General Motors' headquarters refuse to pay a high price for a new means of making high-strength ceramic engines dreamed up by a team of engineers affiliated with Carnegie-Mellon University in Pittsburgh, the strategic brokers of Honda or Mercedes-Benz are likely to be more than willing.

So, too, with the insights of America's ubiquitous management consultants, which are being sold for large sums to eager entrepreneurs in Europe and Latin America. Also, the insights of America's energy consultants, sold for even larger sums to Arab sheikhs. American design engineers are providing insights to Olivetti, Mazda, Siemens, and other global webs; American marketers, techniques for learning what worldwide consumers will buy; American advertisers, ploys for ensuring that they actually do. American architects are issuing designs and blueprints for opera houses, art galleries, museums, luxury hotels, and residential complexes in the world's major cities; American commercial property developers, marketing these properties to worldwide investors and purchasers. . . .

Almost everyone around the world is buying the skills and Insights of Americans who manipulate oral and visual symbols—musicians, sound engineers, film producers, makeup artists, directors, cinematographers, actors and actresses, boxers, scriptwriters, songwriters, and set designers. Among the wealthiest of symbolic analysts are Steven Spielberg, Bill Cosby, Charles Schulz, Eddie Murphy, Sylvester Stallone, Madonna, and other star directors and performers—who are almost as well known on the streets of Dresden and Tokyo as in the Back Bay of Boston. Less well rewarded but no less renowned are the unctuous anchors on Turner Broadcasting's Cable News, who appear daily, via satellite, in places ranging from Vietnam to Nigeria. Vanna White is the world's most watched game-show hostess. Behind each of these familiar faces is a collection of American problem-solvers, -identifiers, and brokers who train, coach, advise, promote, amplify, direct, groom, represent, and otherwise add value to their talents.

There are also the insights of senior American executives who occupy the world headquarters of global "American" corporations and the national or regional headquarters of global "foreign" corporations. Their insights are duly exported to the rest of the world through the webs of global enterprise. IBM does not export many machines from the United States, for example. Big Blue makes machines all over the globe and services them on the spot. Its prime American exports are symbolic and analytic. From IBM's world headquarters in Armonk, New York, emanate strategic brokerage and related management services bound for the rest of the world. In return, IBM's top executives are generously rewarded.

QUESTIONS

1. According to Reich, how did the distribution of wealth in the United States change between 1960 and 1990?
2. What categories of workers does Reich describe? How did the different groups make their livings? How was the relative importance of these categories changing?
3. How was the globalization of manufacturing affecting the American economy? Who benefitted from globalization? Who did not?

30.2. JOSEPH PERKINS, "OP-ED" (OCTOBER 21, 1994), AND *THE NEW YORK TIMES*, "WHY PROPOSITION 187 WON'T WORK" (NOVEMBER 20, 1994)

In 1994, California voters passed Proposition 187, a measure denying government services to undocumented immigrants. Although courts later invalidated Proposition 187, the initiative ignited a nationwide debate over immigration.

JOSEPH PERKINS: "OP-ED"

No one has been harder on California Gov. Pete Wilson than yours truly. But I have to give the devil his due for his principled stand on illegal immigration.

Specifically, I am referring to the governor's unequivocal support for a state ballot measure that would deny California's 1.6 million illegal immigrants taxpayer-funded education, nonemergency health care, welfare benefits and other public social services.

Wilson has been accused of, among other things, "scapegoating," "xenophobia" and "racism." But this is a patently absurd charge. Proposition 187, titled the "Save Our State" initiative, is favored by Californians across the board.

This was borne out by a recent *Los Angeles Times* survey, which showed that the ballot initiative is supported by a majority of Republicans and Democrats, conservatives and liberals, whites and, most telling of all, Hispanics.

California's legal residents recognize that the financially-strapped state no longer can afford to generously proffer government benefits to persons who steal across this country's border.

As it is, illegal immigrants are eligible for almost as many publicly-funded services as U.S. citizens. Indeed, they can cross the border and have babies at American hospitals at taxpayer expense. They can enroll their kids in American schools tuition-free. They can even get welfare benefits in their children's name.

As Wilson has repeatedly mentioned, illegal immigrants cost his state a net of $5 billion annually. That works out to more than $400 a year added to each California family's tax burden.

Sources: Joseph Perkins, "Op-ed," *San Diego Union Tribune*, October 21, 1994; and Nicholas Kristof "Why Proposition 187 Won't Work," editorial, *New York Times*, November 20, 1994.

The illegal immigrants, themselves, are not to be faulted for taking advantage of Yankee largess. We have only ourselves to blame for devaluing U.S. citizenship, for conferring upon those who come here illegally the same rights and privileges as those who are either native-born Americans or who legally immigrated to this country.

Indeed, nothing is more ludicrous than the designation of so-called "citizen children." These are babies who become U.S. citizens through accident of birth; whose illegal-immigrant mothers happen to bring them into the world in an American maternity ward.

The babies are Americanized by virtue of the 14th Amendment's guarantee that any person born on U.S. soil is automatically a citizen. But when the amendment was ratified in 1868, neither Congress nor the state legislatures were even remotely thinking about future illegal immigrants.

They were thinking about former slaves who were brought to this country against their will, on whose backs the South's agrarian economy was built. Black men and women who were third- and fourth-generation residents of this country, who had no first-hand memories of their native land, but who nonetheless were disenfranchised by their new homeland.

To equate the citizenship rights of emancipated slaves with those of babies born to illegal immigrants is to trivialize the history of slavery in this country.

The emancipated slaves earned their U.S. citizenship by virtue of their longevity in this country and their uncompensated labors. The babies of illegal immigrants have done nothing to merit citizenship, except be born at U.S. taxpayer expense.

The 14th Amendment needs to be rewritten by Congress. American citizenship no longer should be routinely bestowed upon a baby that happens to be born here, but whose parents are foreign citizens. Let the child apply for naturalization at the age of 18. If he or she becomes a U.S. citizen then, it will be by intent rather than by default, the way it is now. . . .

America continues to admit more foreign immigrants than all the other countries in the world combined. As most of these immigrants ultimately settle in California, at considerable expense to the state's taxpayers, it hardly is xenophobic or racist if California residents vote to deny publicly-funded benefits and services to immigrants who have entered the country illegally.

NEW YORK TIMES: "WHY PROPOSITION 187 WON'T WORK"

Proposition 187, the California ballot initiative that deprives illegal immigrants of state services, has quickly been revealed as the inhumane headache its opponents promised it would be.

Already a host of examples of the new measure's inevitable consequences have shown how unlikely it is that its supporters really thought much before casting their votes.

Did they, for example, intend to deprive a child who is a legal resident of treatment for lead poisoning—because his illegal mother is too frightened to bring him to the clinic? One health worker has already encountered this situation, although the law has yet to go into effect.

Did Californians, when they voted to deny illegal immigrants non-emergency medical care, think about the consequences of having people go untreated for communicable diseases, thereby putting whole communities at risk? And did Californians really want the people who run child-welfare agencies to abandon children already abandoned by their parents, or to evict abused children now in foster care?

Health care workers, educators and other public servants are having to think about such issues now. That is one reason why the Los Angeles City Council and school district have vowed not to comply with 187; it is one reason why school principals around the state have rushed to reassure their pupils that they have no intention of playing enforcer for the Immigration and Naturalization Service; it is one reason why staffs at health clinics have vowed to give up state funding rather than turn away people in need. . . .

Californians are learning that getting tough with illegal immigrants may sound wonderful in the abstract but it is heartbreaking, and tortuously complicated, in practice. Both because of its inhumanity and its impracticality, Proposition 187 invites massive civil disobedience. It is a bad law, which, if the courts continue to rule wisely, will never have to be instituted.

QUESTIONS

1. On what grounds did each side base its case for or against Proposition 187?
2. What, according to Perkins, should make someone a citizen of the United States? What might be the implications of his goal to rewrite the Fourteenth Amendment?

30.3. DANIEL S. MORROW, INTERVIEW WITH STEVE JOBS (1995)

In 1984, Apple Computer Company introduced the Macintosh, or Mac, a personal computer, designed for easy use and graphic publication. In 1995, Steve Jobs, one of the inventors of the Mac and founders of Apple, explained aspects of the innovative culture of Silicon Valley.

INTRODUCING MACINTOSH. WHAT MAKES IT TICK. AND TALK.

Well, to begin with, 110 volts of alternating current.

Secondly, some of the hottest hardware to come down the pike in the last 3 years.

Some hard facts may be in order at this point:

Macintosh's brain is the same blindingly-fast 32-bit microprocessor we gave our other brainchild, the Lisa™ Personal Computer. Far more powerful than the 16-bit 8088 found in current generation computers.

Its heart is the same Lisa Technology of windows, pull-down menus, mouse commands and icons. All of which make that 32-bit power far more useful by making the Macintosh™ Personal Computer far easier to use than current generation computers. In fact, if you can point without hurting yourself, you can use it.

NOW FOR SOME SMALL TALK.

Thanks to its size, if you can't bring the problem to a Macintosh, you can always bring a Macintosh to the

Steve Jobs (left) and Steve Wozniak (right), the co-founders of Apple. Sal Veder/Associated Press

Source: *Personal Computing*, April 1984, pp. 196–97; Computerworld Honors Program International Archives, "Steve Jobs: Oral History," interview with Daniel S. Morrow, April 20, 1995.

problem. (It weighs 9 pounds less than the most popular "portable.")

Another miracle of miniaturization is Macintosh's built-in 3½" drive. Its disks store 400K—more than conventional 5¼" floppies. So while they're big enough to hold a desk full of work, they're small enough to fit in a shirt pocket. And, they're totally encased in a rigid plastic so they're totally protected.

AND TALK ABOUT PROGRAMMING.

There are already plenty of programs to keep a Macintosh busy. Like MacPaint™, a program that, for the first time, lets a personal computer produce virtually any image the human hand can create. There's more software on the way from developers like Microsoft,* Lotus™, and Software Publishing Corp., to mention a few.

And with Macintosh BASIC, Macintosh Pascal and our Macintosh Toolbox for writing your own mouse-driven programs, you, too, could make big bucks in your spare time.

You can even program Macintosh to talk in other languages, like Yiddish or Serbo-Croatian, because it has a built-in polyphonic sound generator capable of producing high quality speech or music.

ALL THE RIGHT CONNECTIONS.

On the back of the machine, you'll find built-in RS232 and RS422 AppleBus serial communication ports. Which means you can connect printers, modems and other peripherals without adding $150 cards. It also means that Macintosh is ready to hook in to a local area network. (With AppleBus, you will be able to interconnect up to 16 different Apple computers and peripherals.)

Should you wish to double Macintosh's storage with an external disk drive, you can do so without paying for a disk controller card—that connector's built-in, too.

There's also a built-in connector for Macintosh's mouse, a feature that costs up to $300 on computers that can't even run mouse-controlled software.

ONE LAST POINTER.

Now that you've seen some of the logic, the technology, the engineering genius and the software wizardry that separates Macintosh from conventional computers, we'd like to point you in the direction of your nearest authorized Apple dealer.

Over 1500 of them are eagerly waiting to put a mouse in your hand. As one point-and-click makes perfectly clear, the real genius of Macintosh isn't its 32-bit Lisa Technology, or its 3½" floppy disks, or its serial ports, or its software, or its polyphonic sound generator.

The real genius is that you don't have to be a genius to use a Macintosh.

You just have to be smart enough to buy one.

Soon there'll be just two kinds of people. Those who use computers. And those who use Apples.

STEVE JOBS

ORAL HISTORY

COMPUTERWORLD HONORS PROGRAM

INTERNATIONAL ARCHIVES

TRANSCRIPT OF A VIDEO HISTORY

INTERVIEW WITH STEVE JOBS

CO-FOUNDER, APPLE & NEXT COMPUTER

Interviewer: Daniel S. Morrow (DSM)
Executive Director
Computerworld Honors Program
Date: April 20, 1995
Location: NEXT Computer

SJ: Apple was this incredible journey. I mean we did some amazing things there. The thing that bound us together at Apple was the ability to make things that were going to change the world. That was very important. We were all pretty young. The average age in the company was mid-to-late twenties. Hardly anybody had families at the beginning and we all worked like maniacs and the greatest joy was that we felt we were fashioning collective works of art much like twentieth century physics.

Something important that would last, that people contributed to and then could give to more people; the amplification factor was very large. . . .

From almost the beginning at Apple we were, for some incredibly lucky reason, fortunate enough to be at the right place at the right time. The contributions we tried to make embodied values not only of technical excellence and innovation—which I think we did our share of—but innovation of a more humanistic kind.

The things I'm most proud about at Apple is where the technical and the humanistic came together, as it did in publishing for example. The Macintosh basically revolutionized publishing and printing. The typographic artistry coupled with the technical understanding and excellence to implement that electronically—those two things came together and empowered people to use the computer without having to understand arcane computer commands. . . .

DSM: You used an interesting word in describing what you were doing. You were talking about art, not engineering, not science. Tell me about that.

SJ: I actually think there's actually very little distinction between an artist and a scientist or engineer of the highest caliber. I've never had a distinction in my mind between those two types of people. They've just been to me people who pursue different paths but basically kind of headed to the same goal which is to express something of what they perceive to be the truth around them so that others can benefit by it.

DSM: And the artistry is in the elegance of the solution, like chess playing or mathematics?

SJ: . . . If you study these people a little bit more what you'll find is that in this particular time, in the 70's and the 80's the best people in computers

would have normally been poets and writers and musicians. Almost all of them were musicians. A lot of them were poets on the side. They went into computers because it was so compelling. It was fresh and new. It was a new medium of expression for their creative talents. The feelings and the passion that people put into it were completely indistinguishable from a poet or a painter. Many of the people were introspective, inward people who expressed how they felt about other people or the rest of humanity in general into their work, work that other people would use.

QUESTIONS

1. What, to judge from the Macintosh ad, were the characteristics and values of someone who would buy and use a Mac?

2. What, according to Jobs, was the purpose of work for those who created the culture of innovation that led to Apple and Silicon Valley? Does the Macintosh ad reflect these individuals' concept of work's purpose? If so, how so? If not, why not?

3. How did these technological innovators envision the future of computing?

30.4. PRESIDENT CLINTON, EXCERPTS FROM "THE ERA OF BIG GOVERNMENT IS OVER" (JANUARY 23, 1996)

In the 1994 elections, Republicans gained control of both houses of Congress for the first time in forty years. Democratic President Bill Clinton and the Republican congressional majority fought bitterly in 1995, leading to a shutdown of the federal government in the fall. In his 1996 State of the Union address, President Clinton agreed with Republicans that "the era of big government is over," but he also challenged Congress to balance the federal budget.

The state of the Union is strong. Our economy is the healthiest it has been in three decades. We have the lowest combined rates of unemployment and inflation in 27 years. We have completed—created nearly 8 million new jobs, over a million of them in

basic industries like construction and automobiles. America is selling more cars than Japan for the first time since the 1970's. And for 3 years in a row, we have had a record number of new businesses started in our country.

Source: New York Times, January 24, 1996

Our leadership in the world is also strong, bringing hope for new peace. And perhaps most important, we are gaining ground in restoring our fundamental values. The crime rate, the welfare and food stamp rolls, the poverty rate, and the teen pregnancy rate are all down. And as they go down, prospects for America's future go up.

We live in an age of possibility. A hundred years ago we moved from farm to factory. Now we move to an age of technology, information, and global competition. These changes have opened vast new opportunities for our people, but they have also presented them with stiff challenges. While more Americans are living better, too many of our fellow citizens are working harder just to keep up, and they are rightly concerned about the security of their families.

We must answer here three fundamental questions: First, how do we make the American dream of opportunity for all a reality for all Americans who are willing to work for it? Second, how do we preserve our old and enduring values as we move into the future? And third, how do we meet these challenges together, as one America?

We know big Government does not have all the answers. We know there's not a program for every problem. We know, and we have worked to give the American people a smaller, less bureaucratic Government in Washington. And we have to give the American people one that lives within its means. The era of big Government is over. But we cannot go back to the time when our citizens were left to fend for themselves.

Instead, we must go forward as one America, one nation working together to meet the challenges we face together. Self-reliance and teamwork are not opposing virtues; we must have both. I believe our new, smaller Government must work in an old-fashioned American way, together with all of our citizens through State and local governments, in the workplace, in religious, charitable, and civic associations. Our goal must be to enable all our people to make the most of their own lives, with stronger families, more educational opportunity, economic security, safer streets, a cleaner environment in a safer world. . . .

Here, in this place, our responsibility begins with balancing the budget in a way that is fair to all Americans. There is now broad bipartisan agreement that permanent deficit spending must come to an end.

I compliment the Republican leadership and the membership for the energy and determination you have brought to this task of balancing the budget. And I thank the Democrats for passing the largest deficit reduction plan in history in 1993, which has already cut the deficit nearly in half in 3 years.

Since 1993, we have all begun to see the benefits of deficit reduction. Lower interest rates have made it easier for businesses to borrow and to invest and to create new jobs. Lower interest rates have brought down the cost of home mortgages, car payments, and credit card rates to ordinary citizens. Now, it is time to finish the job and balance the budget.

QUESTIONS

1. What, according to Clinton, was the proper role of government now that the era of big government was over?
2. This was Clinton's last State of the Union speech before the presidential election of 1996. In what ways does this speech reflect that impending event?

30.5. *THE ECONOMIST,* "THE END?" (FEBRUARY 11, 1999)

President Bill Clinton's involvement with Monica Lewinsky, a twenty-one-year-old White House intern, captured public attention at home and abroad for a year beginning in January 1998. Britain's *Economist* magazine expressed both the widespread fascination with the subject and the ultimate judgment that Clinton's critics went too far in impeaching the president.

As *The Economist* went to press, it was uncertain exactly how the Senate trial would be brought to its inevitably dismal end. But two things were clear. First, what has happened over the past year should never have happened at all; second, there is no guarantee that it will not happen again. The end of this awful tale still leaves in place the elements that spawned it: a diminished presidency, a bitterly divided Congress, an over-mighty prosecutor, and a media pack that is proud to seek out scandal wherever it can.

It was clear, if not from the start then soon after, that the president's impeachment should never have been undertaken. This huge, ponderous machine, whose workings paralyse normal government, should be activated only to remove a president who is agreed by both political parties and by the people to be a menace to the country. Bill Clinton's offences, perjury and obstruction of justice—not, it bears repeating, that he had a tawdry sexual fling—were in our view grave and shameful. Mr. Clinton disguised private lapses of behaviour with public lying, which had the public consequence of destroying the people's trust in him. To this, the proper response of a man of honour would have been to resign his office. But that was never the view of most Americans; still less did most Americans feel that these crimes justified the president's removal by another branch of government.

Since Mr. Clinton would not go, his political enemies determined to root him out, using impeachment to try to overturn, by a sort of constitutional *coup d'état,* the result of two elections. This is not impeachment's

purpose, and no one has emerged from the process untarnished: not the president, who refused even the courtesy of answering senators' questions, nor the Republican trial managers, who often exhibited pure vengeance, nor the Democrats, whose scramble to embrace their president suggests a wholesale abandonment of principle. It is expected (though nobody can be sure) that the Republicans will reap the whirlwind in the elections of 2000—that they, not the president or his Democrat apologists, will be blamed for taking the country through this horror. Even so, impeachment once devalued may be used this way again, not least by those who feel that vengeance and partisanship are most neatly countered by more of the same.

Morning-after Washington also bears the scars of other excesses. The scandal saw a sort of Faustian pact between the special prosecutor, Ken Starr, and the press, whereby each seemed to feed and encourage the prurient appetites of the other. Mr. Starr's powers to investigate the president had long been condemned as too far-reaching. But when the inquiry turned to sex, rather than obscure tracts of scrubland in Arkansas, the press became insatiable, and Mr. Starr obliged them with an extraordinary flood of detail. Where the Internet dared, the old press followed. Rumour was published before it had been verified; the prosecutor's office sprang leaks for which no apology was offered; and Congress, when the time came, pushed titillating material immediately and unthinkingly into the public domain. This howling after sex stoked the fires

Source: The Economist, "The End," February 11, 1999.

of Republican moralists, obscured the valid reasons for condemning this president, and made the public think one thing: this prosecution was unfair.

HUNGRY PRESS, HUNGRY PROSECUTOR

There is a grain of truth in that. No other president has faced a man of Mr. Starr's resources and persistence (a persistence that is still unsated); and none has had to deal with such a torrent of explicit revelations. Perhaps Mr. Clinton's successors will not have to. In the present mood of national regret, the overwhelming wish never to go through *that* again, the office of the special prosecutor may well be eliminated before the year is out. Yet something will have to replace it; the executive cannot go unwatched. The press will be restrained for a while, no doubt. Yet the modern trend to keep close tabs on the powerful, to comb through their private lives, to expose them and pull them down, is not about to disappear. Every would-be presidential contender now working the malls of New Hampshire must expect to have to defend himself.

The fact is that during the presidency of Bill Clinton, the perception of the office has changed and its authority has diminished. At this point in history,

it is said, America does not require a leader to admire; prosperous and peaceful, it needs only a man who can steer straight, and Mr. Clinton can do that capably enough. Respect and special treatment are not necessary. This attitude was both confirmed and reflected during the Lewinsky affair, by the Supreme Court ruling that the Paula Jones civil suit could proceed against Mr. Clinton while he was in office. But this ruling was misguided; this, too, should not have happened. A president in office is not an ordinary man, but the head of state of the most powerful country on earth. He represents an entity to which, above all, the world looks for guidance. His accountability as a man before the law must always be balanced by a sense of the importance of the office he occupies.

QUESTIONS

1. Did someone or something, in the view of the *Economist*, bear a disproportionate share of the blame for the impeachment of Clinton? If so, who or what? If not, why not?

2. What did the *Economist* see as the likely future of American politics?

CHAPTER 31

TWENTY-FIRST-CENTURY DANGERS AND PROMISES, 2001 TO PRESENT

31.1. AL-QAEDA, *FATWA* AGAINST THE UNITED STATES (FEBRUARY 23, 1998)

In 1998, Osama bin Laden issued a *fatwa*, or religious decree, calling on Muslims to kill Americans and their allies. Few outside intelligence agencies paid close attention to bin Laden until al-Qaeda operatives flew airplanes into the World Trade Center and the Pentagon on September 11, 2001. The United States responded to these attacks with a global war on terror, which included prolonged and costly wars in Iraq and Afghanistan.

Praise be to God, who revealed the Book, controls the clouds, defeats factionalism, and says in His Book: "But when the forbidden months are past, then fight and slay the pagans wherever ye find them, seize them, beleaguer them, and lie in wait for them in every stratagem (of war)"; and peace be upon our Prophet, Muhammad Bin-'Abdallah, who said: I have been sent with the sword between my hands to ensure that no one but God is worshipped, God who put my livelihood under the shadow of my spear and who inflicts humiliation and scorn on those who disobey my orders.

The Arabian Peninsula has never—since God made it flat, created its desert, and encircled it with seas—been stormed by any forces like the crusader armies spreading in it like locusts, eating its riches and wiping out its plantations. All this is happening at a time in which nations are attacking Muslims like people fighting over a plate of food. In the light of the grave situation and the lack of support, we and you are obliged to discuss current events, and we should all agree on how to settle the matter.

No one argues today about three facts that are known to everyone; we will list them, in order to remind everyone:

First, for over seven years the United States has been occupying the lands of Islam in the holiest of places, the Arabian Peninsula, plundering its riches, dictating to its rulers, humiliating its people, terrorizing its neighbors, and turning its bases in the Peninsula into a spearhead through which to fight the neighboring Muslim peoples.

If some people have in the past argued about the fact of the occupation, all the people of the Peninsula have now acknowledged it. The best proof of this is

Source: "Al Qaeda's Fatwa," *Newshour with Jim Lehrer*, February 23, 1998, http://www.pbs.org/newshour/terrorism/international/fatwa_1998.html

the Americans' continuing aggression against the Iraqi people using the Peninsula as a staging post, even though all its rulers are against their territories being used to that end, but they are helpless.

Second, despite the great devastation inflicted on the Iraqi people by the crusader-Zionist alliance, and despite the huge number of those killed, which has exceeded 1 million . . . despite all this, the Americans are once again trying to repeat the horrific massacres, as though they are not content with the protracted blockade imposed after the ferocious war or the fragmentation and devastation.

So here they come to annihilate what is left of this people and to humiliate their Muslim neighbors. Third, if the Americans' aims behind these wars are religious and economic, the aim is also to serve the Jews' petty state and divert attention from its occupation of Jerusalem and murder of Muslims there. The best proof of this is their eagerness to destroy Iraq, the strongest neighboring Arab state, and their endeavor to fragment all the states of the region such as Iraq, Saudi Arabia, Egypt, and Sudan into paper statelets and through their disunion and weakness to guarantee Israel's survival and the continuation of the brutal crusade occupation of the Peninsula. . . .

The ruling to kill the Americans and their allies—civilians and military—is an individual duty for every Muslim who can do it in any country in which it is possible to do it, in order to liberate the al-Aqsa Mosque and the holy mosque [Mecca] from their grip, and in order for their armies to move out of all the lands of Islam, defeated and unable to threaten any Muslim. This is in accordance with the words of Almighty God, "and fight the pagans all together as they fight you all together," and "fight them until there is no more tumult or oppression, and there prevail justice and faith in God." . . .

We—with God's help—call on every Muslim who believes in God and wishes to be rewarded to comply with God's order to kill the Americans and plunder their money wherever and whenever they find it. We also call on Muslim ulema, leaders, youths, and soldiers to launch the raid on Satan's U.S. troops and the devil's supporters allying with them, and to displace those who are behind them so that they may learn a lesson. . . .

Almighty God also says: "O ye who believe, what is the matter with you, that when ye are asked to go forth in the cause of God, ye cling so heavily to the earth! Do ye prefer the life of this world to the hereafter? But little is the comfort of this life, as compared with the hereafter. Unless ye go forth, He will punish you with a grievous penalty, and put others in your place; but Him ye would not harm in the least. For God hath power over all things."

Almighty God also says: "So lose no heart, nor fall into despair. For ye must gain mastery if ye are true in faith."

QUESTIONS

1. What, in bin Laden's view, justified his *fatwa* against the United States?
2. What did bin Laden hope to achieve by issuing this *fatwa*?

31.2. KENNETH ADELMAN, "CAKEWALK IN IRAQ" (FEBRUARY 13, 2002)

Soon after the terror attacks of September 11, 2001, officials of the Bush administration advocated a U.S. assault on Iraq to destroy the regime of Saddam Hussein and create a democracy that would be a model for other states in the Arab Middle East. Critics of the plan advised caution, because they predicted that a war against Iraq would be prolonged and costly. Kenneth Adelman, a supporter of a war with Iraq, explains why he believes such a war would be short and inexpensive.

Even before President Bush had placed Iraq on his "axis of evil," dire warnings were being sounded about the danger of acting against Saddam Hussein's regime. Two knowledgeable Brookings Institution analysts, Philip H. Gordon and Michael E. O'Hanlon, concluded that the United States would "almost

Source: Kenneth Adelman, "Cakewalk in Iraq," *Washington Post*, February 13, 2002, A27.

surely" need "at least 100,000 to 200,000" ground forces [op-ed, December 26, 2001]. Worse: "Historical precedents from Panama to Somalia to the Arab–Israeli wars suggest that . . . the United States could lose thousands of troops in the process."

I agree that taking down Hussein would differ from taking down the Taliban. And no one favors "a casual march to war." This is serious business, to be treated seriously.

In fact, we took it seriously the last time such fear-mongering was heard from military analysts—when we considered war against Iraq 11 years ago. Edward N. Luttwak cautioned on the eve of Desert Storm: "All those precision weapons and gadgets and gizmos and stealth fighters . . . are not going to make it possible to re-conquer Kuwait without many thousands of casualties." As it happened, our gizmos worked wonders. Luttwak's estimate of casualties was off by "many thousands," just as the current estimates are likely to be.

I believe demolishing Hussein's military power and liberating Iraq would be a cakewalk. Let me give simple, responsible reasons: (1) It was a cakewalk last time; (2) they've become much weaker; (3) we've become much stronger; and (4) now we're playing for keeps.

Gordon and O'Hanlon mention today's "400,000 active-duty troops in the Iraqi military" and especially the "100,000 in Saddam's more reliable Republican Guard and Special Republican Guard," which "would probably fight hard against the United States—just as they did a decade ago during Desert Storm." Somehow I missed that. I do remember a gaggle of Iraqi troops attempting to surrender to an Italian film crew. The bulk of the vaunted Republican Guard either hunkered down or was held back from battle.

Today Iraqi forces are much weaker. Saddam's army is one-third its size then, in both manpower and number of divisions. It still relies on obsolete Soviet tanks, which military analyst Eliot Cohen calls "death traps." The Iraqi air force, never much, is half its former size.

Iraqi forces have received scant spare parts and no weapons upgrades. They have undertaken little operational training since Desert Storm.

Meanwhile, American power is much fiercer. The advent of precision bombing and battlefield intelligence has dramatically spiked U.S. military prowess.

The gizmos of Desert Storm were 90-plus percent dumb bombs. Against the Taliban, more than 80 percent were smart bombs. Unmanned Predators equipped with Hellfire missiles and Global Hawk intelligence gathering did not exist during the first Iraqi campaign.

In 1991 we engaged a grand international coalition because we lacked a domestic coalition. Virtually the entire Democratic leadership stood against that President Bush. The public, too, was divided. This President Bush does not need to amass rinky-dink nations as "coalition partners" to convince the Washington establishment that we're right. Americans of all parties now know we must wage a total war on terrorism.

Hussein constitutes the number one threat against American security and civilization. Unlike Osama bin Laden, he has billions of dollars in government funds, scores of government research labs working feverishly on weapons of mass destruction—and just as deep a hatred of America and civilized free societies.

Once President Bush clearly announces that our objective is to rid Iraq of Hussein, and our unshakable determination to do whatever it takes to win, defections from the Iraqi army may come even faster than a decade ago.

Gordon and O'Hanlon say we must not "assume that Hussein will quickly fall." I think that's just what is likely to happen. How would it be accomplished? By knocking out all his headquarters, communications, air defenses and fixed military facilities through precision bombing. By establishing military "no-drive zones" wherever Iraqi forces try to move. By arming the Kurds in the north, Shiites in the south and his many opponents everywhere. By using U.S. special forces and some U.S. ground forces with protective gear against chemical and biological weapons. By stationing theater missile defenses, to guard against any Iraqi Scuds still in existence. And by announcing loudly that any Iraqi, of any rank, who handles Hussein's weapons of mass destruction, in any form, will be severely punished after the war.

Measured by any cost–benefit analysis, such an operation would constitute the greatest victory in America's war on terrorism.

The writer was assistant to Defense Secretary Donald Rumsfeld from 1975 to 1977, and arms control director under President Ronald Reagan.

QUESTIONS

1. What promised to make war against Iraq a "cakewalk," in Adelman's view?

2. Adelman links a war on Iraq to a wider war on terrorism. What evidence does Adelman provide to establish such a link?

31.3. JUSTICE JOHN PAUL STEVENS, EXCERPTS FROM *HAMDAN V. RUMSFELD* (JUNE 29, 2006)

During the war on terror, U.S. forces captured hundreds of "enemy combatants" around the world and imprisoned them at a military base in Guantanamo Bay, Cuba. In 2006, the Supreme Court ruled that the military commission established by President George W. Bush to try captives was unconstitutional.

Justice Stevens announced the judgment of the Court and delivered the opinion of the Court with respect to Parts I through IV, Parts VI through VI-D-iii, Part VI-D-v, and Part VII, and an opinion with respect to Parts V and VI-D-iv, in which Justice Souter, Justice Ginsburg, and Justice Breyer join.

Petitioner Salim Ahmed Hamdan, a Yemeni national, is in custody at an American prison in Guantanamo Bay, Cuba. In November 2001, during hostilities between the United States and the Taliban (which then governed Afghanistan), Hamdan was captured by militia forces and turned over to the U.S. military. In June 2002, he was transported to Guantanamo Bay. Over a year later, the President deemed him eligible for trial by military commission for then-unspecified crimes. After another year had passed, Hamdan was charged with one count of conspiracy "to commit . . . offenses triable by military commission." App. to Pet. for Cert. 65a.

Hamdan filed petitions for writs of habeas corpus and mandamus to challenge the Executive Branch's intended means of prosecuting this charge. He concedes that a court-martial constituted in accordance with the Uniform Code of Military Justice (UCMJ), 10 U.S.C. §801 *et seq.* (2000 ed. and Supp. III), would have authority to try him. His objection is that the military commission the President has convened lacks such authority, for two principal reasons: First, neither congressional Act nor the common law of war supports trial by this commission for the crime of conspiracy—an offense that, Hamdan says, is not a violation of the law of war. Second, Hamdan contends, the procedures that the President has adopted to try him violate the most basic tenets of military and international law, including the principle that a defendant must be permitted to see and hear the evidence against him.

The District Court granted Hamdan's request for a writ of habeas corpus. 344 F. Supp. 2d 152 (DC 2004). The Court of Appeals for the District of Columbia Circuit reversed. 415 F. 3d 33 (2005). Recognizing, as we did over a half-century ago, that trial by military commission is an extraordinary measure raising important questions about the balance of powers in our constitutional structure, *Ex parte Quirin*, 317 U.S. 1, 19 (1942), we granted certiorari. 546 U.S. _____ (2005).

For the reasons that follow, we conclude that the military commission convened to try Hamdan lacks power to proceed because its structure and procedures violate both the UCMJ and the Geneva Conventions. Four of us also conclude, see Part V, *infra*, that the offense with which Hamdan has been charged is not an "offens[e] that by . . . the law of war may be tried by military commissions." 10 U.S.C. §821. . . . Common Article 3 obviously tolerates a great degree of flexibility in trying individuals captured during armed conflict; its requirements are general ones, crafted to accommodate a wide variety of legal systems. But *requirements* they are nonetheless. The commission that the President has convened to try Hamdan does not meet those requirements. . . . We have assumed, as we must, that the allegations made in the Government's charge

Source: Cornell University Law School Legal Information Institute, http://www.law.cornell.edu/supct/html/05–184.ZO.html

against Hamdan are true. We have assumed, moreover, the truth of the message implicit in that charge—viz., that Hamdan is a dangerous individual whose beliefs, if acted upon, would cause great harm and even death to innocent civilians, and who would act upon those beliefs if given the opportunity. It bears emphasizing that Hamdan does not challenge, and we do not today address, the Government's power to detain him for the duration of active hostilities in order to prevent such harm. But in undertaking to try Hamdan and subject him to criminal punishment, the Executive is bound to comply with the Rule of Law that prevails in this jurisdiction.

The judgment of the Court of Appeals is reversed, and the case is remanded for further proceedings.

It is so ordered.

The Chief Justice took no part in the consideration or decision of this case.

QUESTIONS

1. On what grounds did the court find the military commission that was supposed to try Hamdan to be unconstitutional?
2. Did the court majority believe balance of powers to be the most important issue at stake in the Hamdan case? If so, why? If not, why not?

31.4. POPE JOHN PAUL II, ROBERT AND MARY SCHINDLER, JUDGE GEORGE GREER, AND THE FLORIDA COURT OF APPEALS: OPINIONS ON TERRI SCHIAVO AND THE RIGHT TO DIE (2000s)

Arguments over the morality and legality of removing a feeding tube from Terri Schiavo became a flashpoint in the culture wars of the 1990s. Terri Schiavo's husband, Michael Schiavo, argued for the right to remove a feeding tube from his wife because she was in a persistent vegetative state. Her parents, Robert and Mary Schindler, argued that her Roman Catholic faith banned the use of any means to shorten life. Florida Judge George Greer repeatedly ruled in favor of Michael Schiavo, Terri's guardian.

POPE JOHN PAUL II

Faced with patients in similar clinical conditions, there are some who cast doubt on the persistence of the "human quality" itself, almost as if the adjective "vegetative" (whose use is now solidly established), which symbolically describes a clinical state, could or should be instead applied to the sick as such, actually demeaning their value and personal dignity. In this sense, it must be noted that this term, even when confined to the clinical context, is certainly not the most felicitous when applied to human beings. . . . In opposition to such trends of thought, I feel the duty to reaffirm strongly that the intrinsic value and personal dignity of every human being do not change, no matter what the concrete circumstances of his or her life. *A man, even if seriously ill or disabled in the exercise of his highest functions, is and always will be a man,* and he will never become a "vegetable" or an "animal." . . . Even our brothers and sisters who find themselves in the clinical condition of a "vegetative state" retain their human dignity in all its fullness.

ROBERT AND MARY SCHINDLER

Mrs. Schiavo's medical condition in February 2000 was misrepresented to the trial court and to this court

Sources: John Paul II, Address to the World Federation of Catholic Medical Associations and Pontifical Academy for Life Congress, March 2004, http://www.vatican.va/holy_father/john_paul_ii/speeches/2004/march/documents/hf_jp-ii_spe_20040320_congressfiamc_en.html; and Kenneth W. Goodman, *The Case of Terri Schiavo: Ethics, Politics, and Death in the 21st Century* (New York: Oxford University Press, 2010), 27, 83, 171–73.

throughout these proceedings. They claim that she is not in a persistent vegetative state. What is more important, they maintain that current accepted medical treatment exists to restore her ability to eat and speak. The initial trial focused on what Mrs. Schiavo would have decided given her current medical condition and not on whether any available medical treatment could improve her condition. The Schindlers argue that in light of this new evidence of additional medical procedures intended to improve her condition, Mrs. Schiavo would now elect to undergo new treatment and would reverse the prior decision to withdraw life-prolonging procedures.

JUDGE GEORGE GREER

[It is] beyond all doubt that [Mrs. Schiavo] is in a persistent vegetative state . . . per the specific testimony of Dr. James Barnhill and corroborated by Dr. Vincent Gambone. The medical evidence before this court conclusively establishes that she has no hope of ever regaining consciousness and therefore capacity. . . . The film offered into evidence by [the Schindlers] does nothing to change these medical opinions which are supported by the CAT scans in evidence. Mrs. Schindler has testified as her perceptions [sic] regarding her daughter and the court is not unmindful that perceptions may become reality to the person having them. But the overwhelming credible evidence is that Terri Schiavo has been totally unresponsive since lapsing into the coma almost ten years ago, that her movements are reflexive and predicated on brain stem activity alone, that she suffers from severe structural brain damage and to a large extent her brain has been replaced by spinal fluid, that with the exception of one witness whom the court finds to be so biased as to lack credibility, her movements are occasional and totally consistent with the testimony of the expert medical witnesses.

FLORIDA COURT OF APPEALS

The evidence is overwhelming that Theresa is in a permanent or persistent vegetative state. It is important to understand that a persistent vegetative state is not simply a coma. She is not asleep. She has cycles of apparent wakefulness and apparent sleep without any cognition or awareness. As she breathes, she often makes moaning sounds. . . . Over the span of this last decade, Theresa's brain has deteriorated because of the lack of oxygen it suffered at the time of the heart attack.

QUESTIONS

1. For what reasons did Pope John Paul II and the Schindlers oppose the removal of Terri Schiavo's feeding tube? Why did Judge Greer and the Florida Court of Appeals refuse their claim?
2. What made this case so controversial and so reflective of the cultural divides then present in the United States?

31.5. TEXT OF PRESIDENT OBAMA'S SPEECH IN HIROSHIMA, JAPAN, MAY 2016

The following is a transcript of President Obama's speech in Hiroshima, Japan, as recorded by the *New York Times*.[1]

May 27, 2016

Seventy-one years ago, on a bright cloudless morning, death fell from the sky and the world was changed. A flash of light and a wall of fire destroyed a city and demonstrated that mankind possessed the means to destroy itself.

Why do we come to this place, to Hiroshima? We come to ponder a terrible force unleashed in a not-so-distant past. We come to mourn the dead, including over 100,000 Japanese men, women and children, thousands of Koreans, a dozen Americans held prisoner.

1. A version of this article appeared in print on May 28, 2016, on page A8 of the New York edition with the headline, "The Memory of the Morning of Aug. 6, 1945, Must Never Fade." © 2016 The New York Times Company.

Their souls speak to us. They ask us to look inward, to take stock of who we are and what we might become.

It is not the fact of war that sets Hiroshima apart. Artifacts tell us that violent conflict appeared with the very first man. Our early ancestors having learned to make blades from flint and spears from wood used these tools not just for hunting but against their own kind. On every continent, the history of civilization is filled with war, whether driven by scarcity of grain or hunger for gold, compelled by nationalist fervor or religious zeal. Empires have risen and fallen. Peoples have been subjugated and liberated. And at each juncture, innocents have suffered, a countless toll, their names forgotten by time.

The world war that reached its brutal end in Hiroshima and Nagasaki was fought among the wealthiest and most powerful of nations. Their civilizations had given the world great cities and magnificent art. Their thinkers had advanced ideas of justice and harmony and truth. And yet the war grew out of the same base instinct for domination or conquest that had mused conflicts among the simplest tribes, an old pattern amplified by new capabilities and without new constraints.

In the span of a few years, some 60 million people would die. Men, women, children, no different than us. Shot, beaten, marched, bombed, jailed, starved, gassed to death. There are many sites around the world that chronicle this war, memorials that tell stories of courage and heroism, graves and empty camps that echo of unspeakable depravity.

Yet in the image of a mushroom cloud that rose into these skies, we are most starkly reminded of humanity's core contradiction. How the very spark that marks us as a species, our thoughts, our imagination, our language, our toolmaking, our ability to set ourselves apart from nature and bend it to our will—those very things also give us the capacity for unmatched destruction.

How often does material advancement or social innovation blind us to this truth? How easily we learn to justify violence in the name of some higher cause.

Every great religion promises a pathway to love and peace and righteousness, and yet no religion has been spared from believers who have claimed their faith as a license to kill.

Nations arise telling a story that binds people together in sacrifice and cooperation, allowing for remarkable feats. But those same stories have so often been used to oppress and dehumanize those who are different.

Science allows us to communicate across the seas and fly above the clouds, to cure disease and understand the cosmos, but those same discoveries can be turned into ever more efficient killing machines.

The wars of the modern age teach us this truth. Hiroshima teaches this truth. Technological progress without an equivalent progress in human institutions can doom us. The scientific revolution that led to the splitting of an atom requires a moral revolution as well.

That is why we come to this place. We stand here in the middle of this city and force ourselves to imagine the moment the bomb fell. We force ourselves to feel the dread of children confused by what they see. We listen to a silent cry. We remember all the innocents killed across the arc of that terrible war and the wars that came before and the wars that would follow.

Mere words cannot give voice to such suffering. But we have a shared responsibility to look directly into the eye of history and ask what we must do differently to curb such suffering again.

Some day, the voices of the hibakusha will no longer be with us to bear witness. But the memory of the morning of Aug. 6, 1945, must never fade. That memory allows us to fight complacency. It fuels our moral imagination. It allows us to change.

And since that fateful day, we have made choices that give us hope. The United States and Japan have forged not only an alliance but a friendship that has won far more for our people than we could ever claim through war. The nations of Europe built a union that replaced battlefields with bonds of commerce and democracy. Oppressed people and nations won liberation. An international community established institutions and treaties that work to avoid war and aspire to restrict and roll back and ultimately eliminate the existence of nuclear weapons.

Still, every act of aggression between nations, every act of terror and corruption and cruelty and oppression that we see around the world shows our work is never done. We may not be able to eliminate man's capacity to do evil, so nations and the alliances that we form must possess the means to defend ourselves. But among those nations like my own that hold nuclear stockpiles, we must have the courage to escape the logic of fear and pursue a world without them.

We may not realize this goal in my lifetime, but persistent effort can roll back the possibility of catastrophe. We can chart a course that leads to the destruction of these stockpiles. We can stop the spread to new nations and secure deadly materials from fanatics.

And yet that is not enough. For we see around the world today how even the crudest rifles and barrel bombs can serve up violence on a terrible scale. We must change our mind-set about war itself. To prevent conflict through diplomacy and strive to end conflicts after they've begun. To see our growing interdependence as a cause for peaceful cooperation and not violent competition. To define our nations not by our capacity to destroy but by what we build. And perhaps, above all, we must reimagine our connection to one another as members of one human race.

For this, too, is what makes our species unique. We're not bound by genetic code to repeat the mistakes of the past. We can learn. We can choose. We can tell our children a different story, one that describes a common humanity, one that makes war less likely and cruelty less easily accepted.

We see these stories in the hibakusha. The woman who forgave a pilot who flew the plane that dropped the atomic bomb because she recognized that what she really hated was war itself. The man who sought out families of Americans killed here because he believed their loss was equal to his own.

My own nation's story began with simple words: All men are created equal and endowed by our creator with certain unalienable rights including life, liberty and the pursuit of happiness. Realizing that ideal has never been easy, even within our own borders, even among our own citizens. But staying true to that story is worth the effort. It is an ideal to be strived for, an ideal that extends across continents and across oceans. The irreducible worth of every person, the insistence that every life is precious, the radical and necessary notion that we are part of a single human family—that is the story that we all must tell.

That is why we come to Hiroshima. So that we might think of people we love. The first smile from our children in the morning. The gentle touch from a spouse over the kitchen table. The comforting embrace of a parent. We can think of those things and know that those same precious moments took place here, 71 years ago.

Those who died, they are like us. Ordinary people understand this, I think. They do not want more war. They would rather that the wonders of science be focused on improving life and not eliminating it. When the choices made by nations, when the choices made by leaders, reflect this simple wisdom, then the lesson of Hiroshima is done.

The world was forever changed here, but today the children of this city will go through their day in peace. What a precious thing that is. It is worth protecting, and then extending to every child. That is a future *we* can choose, a future in which Hiroshima and Nagasaki are known not as the dawn of atomic warfare but as the start of our own moral awakening.

QUESTIONS

1. What new threats to humanity did nuclear weapons pose?
2. How would the destruction of Hiroshima help assure peace?
3. How did Obama explain the use of the atomic bomb in relation to World War II?
4. Why did the president emphasize the risk of future nuclear war?

31.6. EXCERPTS FROM DONALD J. TRUMP'S INAUGURAL ADDRESS (JANUARY 20, 2017)

The following is a transcript of President Trump's inaugural address on January 20, 2017.

We, the citizens of America, are now joined in a great national effort to rebuild our country and to restore its promise for all our people. . . . We will face challenges but we will get the job done. . . .

For too long, a small group in our nation's Capitol has reaped the rewards of government while the people have borne the cost. . . . Politicians prospered—but the jobs left, and factories closed. . . . Their victories have not been your victories . . . but all that changes—starting right here. . . .

January 20, 2017, will be remembered as the day the people became the rulers of this nation again. The Forgotten men and women of our country will be forgotten no longer. Everyone is listening to you now.

. . . But for too many of our citizens, a different reality exists: Mothers and children trapped in poverty in our inner cities; rusted-out factories scattered like tombstones across the landscape of our nation; an education system, flush with cash, but which leaves our young and beautiful students deprived of knowledge; and the crime and gangs and drugs that have stolen too many lives and robbed our country of so much unrealized potential.

This American carnage stops right here and stops right now. . . .

For many decades, we've enriched foreign industry at the expense of American industry; Subsidized the armies of other countries while allowing for the very sad depletion of our military; We've defended other nation's borders while refusing to defend our own. And spent trillions of dollars overseas while America's infrastructure has fallen into disrepair and decay. We've made other countries rich while the wealth, strength, and confidence of our country have disappeared over the horizon. One by one, the factories shuttered and left our shores, with not one thought about the millions upon millions of workers left behind. The wealth of our middle class has been ripped from their homes and then redistributed across the entire world. But that is the past. And now we are looking only to the future. . . .

From this day forward, a new vision will govern our land. From this moment on, it's going to be America First. Every decision on trade, on taxes, on immigration, on foreign affairs, will be made to benefit American workers and American families.

We must protect our borders from the ravages of other countries making our products, stealing our companies, and destroying our jobs. Protection will lead to great prosperity and strength. America will start winning again, winning like never before. We will bring back our jobs. We will bring back our borders. We will bring back our wealth. . . .

We will follow two simple rules: Buy American and Hire American.

We will seek friendship and goodwill with the nations of the world—but we do so with the understanding that it is the right of all nations to put their own interests first. . . .

At the bedrock of our policies will be a total allegiance to the United States of America. . . .

The time for empty talk is over. . . .

You will never be ignored again . . .

Together we will make America strong again.

We will make America wealthy again.

We will make America proud again.

We will make America safe again.

And yes, we will make America Great Again. Thank you, God Bless you, and God Bless America.

QUESTIONS

1. What economic problems did Trump blame on his predecessors? What solutions did he propose?

Source: New York Times, January 21, 2017